PAINTING THE PAST

A GUIDE FOR WRITING HISTORICAL FICTION

MEREDITH ALLARD

Cover design by Robin Ludwig

ISBN: 9780578533841

Painting the Past: A Guide for Writing Historical Fiction/Meredith Allard – 1st paperback edition 2021

{1. Nonfiction. 2. Creative Writing—Nonfiction. 3. Writing Historical Fiction —Nonfiction. 4. Writing Reference—Nonfiction. 5. Authorship—Nonfiction. 6. Creativity Self-Help—Nonfiction.} I. Title

Copperfield Press

www.copperfieldpress.com

"To My Dear and Loving Husband" by Anne Bradstreet is in the public domain.

FOREWORD

I imagine these days some nonfiction books will come with a note, you know, a BCV or PCV denotation—Before COVID-19 or Post COVID-19. *Painting the Past* was mainly written in a Before COVID-19 world but it's being revised while the virus is rearing its ugly head yet again. It's amazing what has changed. Interviewing experts, visiting libraries, traveling for research, heck, even going to the grocery store without a face mask seems quaint now.

Now, thanks to the vaccines, we'll begin to return to a more normal pace of life. We'll travel for leisure and research again, we'll tap into experts' knowledge through face to face interviews, and we'll visit libraries more easily. Since we'll be headed back to that in one form or another, I decided to leave the information that might seem outdated at this exact moment so we can refer to it whenever seems appropriate.

Come to think of it, now may well be the perfect time for historical fiction.

INTRODUCTION

I've had the idea for this book for some time now. *Painting the Past* is a project I've been poking and prodding as I've been making sense of my intention for putting my ideas about writing historical fiction out into the world.

The truth is I'm not a fan of how-to books. I know, but it's true. Look anywhere for writing advice and you'll see a lot of "Top 10 Things To Do If You Want to Write an International Bestseller!" and "Don't Do This Unless You Want Your Book to Die a Slow and Violent Death!" Once I read a post that said never, under any circumstances, should you begin your novel with a funeral. For fun I began my next novel with a funeral because that's the way I roll.

The main reason I'm not a fan of how-to writing books is because often the authors make claims that cannot be substantiated. Declarations about how to create something, anything, ignores the obvious fact that all creators have their own styles, their own visions, their own voices.

There is no one size fits all when it comes to writing historical fiction, or any fiction. There is no one size fits all for any kind of writing, or any art. The key to becoming a writer for the long haul is to discover your own path. That's not easy. It's much easier to let someone else tell you what to do. It's hard to learn to trust yourself, especially when we live in a world where everyone wants to declare themselves an expert and tell you it's my way or the highway. Who wants their book to die a slow and violent death? But if you think about your favorite authors, I bet you'll discover that they are unique. Creative. Willing to break the rules and create their own.

I call this book *a guide for writing historical fiction* since this book is not intended to be the end all, be all of writing historical fiction. My goal is to help writers learn to feel comfortable tapping into their creativity as they discover their own best practices. I want writers to challenge themselves, try new things, especially things that seem crazy at first but might actually work in the end. I want writers to realize, like Dorothy in the *Wizard of Oz*, that they already have the power. And to add more complexity to the mix, what works for one project may not work for the next. Each project will require new imagination, new thoughts, new ideas. A new recipe, if you will.

Did you catch that? There is no one way, and certainly no right way, to write historical fiction. I can, and will, offer tips and tricks for writing historical fiction, but the truth is it's up to each writer to do the work.

You may have noticed that I'm referring to writing historical fiction as an art. I realize that not everyone views writing as an art. Some view it as a job, as an income, as something other than whatever the word "art" conjures. But writing as a career and writing as a creative pursuit are not diametrically opposed. And everyone, no matter why they write, needs inspiration, some reason to get their bottoms into chairs so they can get their stories out of their heads.

I'm not sure where the idea that writing is easy or glamorous came from, but it's not true, at least not for me. Writing is hard, especially the first draft. Staring at a blank page can be paralyzing. How do we discover the ideas, the characters (both real and imagined), the settings, the details, and the structures we need to tell our historical stories? That's where creativity kicks in.

In case you're wondering about me, I'm the founder and executive editor of *The Copperfield Review*, an award-winning literary journal for readers and writers of historical fiction. Due to my work at *Copperfield*, I've read thousands of historical short stories, novel excerpts, novels, and history-based poetry. I've taught workshops in creative writing and writing historical fiction. I also write historical fiction. I've written novels set in eras ranging from Biblical Jerusalem to the Japanese-American internment camps during World War II. The books in my *Loving Husband Trilogy* and the *Hembry Castle Chronicles* have been bestsellers. So I have some experience with historical fiction. A bit.

In this book, I'll share tips I've discovered as an editor of historical fiction. I'll share what I've learned through teaching historical fiction workshops. I'll also share what has worked for me as a historical novelist. Although I'm speaking primarily from the perspective of writing historical novels, much of what I'm sharing can apply to writing historical short fiction as well. My hope is that this guide inspires you to write the historical tale you want to tell.

I should also tell you what this book is not. This book will not cover querying an agent or a publisher. It will not cover self-publishing, traditional publishing, or book marketing. There are many wonderful books about those topics. This book will not tell you how to write a bestselling novel. There is no magic formula for that despite what some might want you to believe. There are too many variables that go into creating a bestseller. Some of those variables are in our control, but some are not. I prefer to focus on what I can control, and the main thing I can control is the story I tell. This book will guide you along the journey of telling your own historical story.

Give in to your daydreams. Do the work. Let your imagination loose into the world so you can share your love of history and your passion for the written word with others.

WHY HISTORICAL FICTION? PART I

History shows us a window into our past. Historical fiction can take us by the hand and lead us into that world.
    ~Judith Geary

How did you find your way to writing historical fiction? For me, and maybe for you too, it stems from my love of reading historical fiction, or reading anything, really.

My mother credits my early reading to the fact that I watched *Sesame Street* as a child. Ernie and Bert and ABC songs aside, books were my first and best friends. I lived in books. In books I saw that there were other worlds, other times, other ways to live besides my frantic childhood home where my father could never hold down a job and we were evicted from every apartment we ever lived in. To escape, I read anything and everything.

I remember sitting in Mrs. McCoy's third grade classroom in Erwin Street Elementary School in Van Nuys, California, there on the blue and red checkered rug near the well-stocked bookcases. I remember Mrs. McCoy watching me as I read while the other kids played. I read *Charlotte's Web*. I read everything by Beverly Cleary. I read the *Little House on the Prairie* books. I discovered Judy Blume. I was always the first student to finish my work, and with my free time I would rush to the bookcases to discover something new to read.

I remember the day, I might have been in fourth grade, when I stayed behind at the lunch tables in the outdoor cafeteria, intent on the book in my hands. The lunch monitor stopped near me and said, "Don't you want to play with the other kids?" I shook my head and returned to my book. I heard the children's laugher while they ran across the blacktop or jumped rope or played tetherball, but I preferred my book. Reading was how I learned about the world. It still is.

My love for historical fiction began in high school when I read Alex Haley's *Roots*, James Clavell's *Shogun,* and anything by John Jakes or Jean M. Auel. My 11th grade English teacher, Mrs. Russell, told me I was a talented writer and I should consider making writing my career—journalism, perhaps? One journalism class was enough for me to see that the "Just the facts, ma'am" style of writing wasn't for me. At university I turned my attention to screenwriting. I was an English major, but I took several screenwriting classes and even worked as a script analyst for a Hollywood film production company. I realized soon enough that screenwriting wasn't for me either.

In TV and film the screenwriter is often the least important person in the process. The screenwriter writes the original script, but the pages are revised so often that the story can become unrecognizable in the end product. Besides, when you write a script you're writing a blueprint with only the most basic descriptions of characters and setting. You need to leave room for the director, the actors, the set designers, the costume designers, and everyone else to do their jobs. I didn't want to write a blueprint. I wanted to describe everything—the characters, their clothes, the setting. I wanted to be the actors, the set designer, the costume designer, the director. I wanted people to see the scenes the way I saw them. After I left my Hollywood job I discovered the joy of writing historical fiction.

There is something fulfilling about writing historical fiction that I haven't found in writing any other genre. Through fictional snapshots, I can take one moment in time and flesh it out by adding characters with recognizable problems. I can share the events of that era and how my characters are affected and rise to the challenge, or not. When I write historical fiction I become a time traveler with one foot in the present and another in the past. Through historical fiction I can connect to times I can never experience for myself, and learning about people's day to day lives—from what they wore to what they ate to how they survived difficult circumstances—makes historical fiction intellectually as well as emotionally satisfying. Historical fiction is, as far as I'm concerned, the best of all worlds.

Here is a Quick Write to get you started on your own journey toward writing historical fiction. A Quick Write is exactly what it sounds like. You're writing quickly, keeping the words coming, for ten minutes. You can keep your Quick Writes together in an electronic journal on your computer or you can keep a handwritten journal. It's entirely up to you.

Quick Write: What do you love to read? Who are your favorite authors? What is it about these authors and their stories that you love?

Keep in mind that if you don't love to read historical fiction, then writing historical fiction is not for you. That goes for writing any genre. Whenever a potential novelist asks me, "What should I write?" I always start by asking, "What do you love to read?" Whatever your answer is to that question, that's what you should write. If you love to read mysteries, write mysteries. If you love to read suspense thrillers, write suspense thrillers. Hopefully, at least one of your answers to the question "What do you love to read?" is historical fiction. Hopefully, at least one of your favorite authors is a historical novelist.

The good news is that historical fiction is a flexible genre. You can write historical romances, historical mysteries, history-inspired fantasies (as in *Game of Thrones*), historical thrillers, and literary historical fiction, just to name a few variations.

WHY HISTORICAL FICTION? PART II

There is no worse agony than bearing an untold story inside you.
  ~Maya Angelou

Quick Write: Why you want to write historical fiction? Why are you drawn to write in this genre, especially when writing historical fiction can be more challenging than other genres?

Be as specific as you can when answering the above questions. The clearer your vision for why you're writing historical fiction, the easier it will be to stay motivated. Do you want to entertain? Enlighten? Educate? Are you fascinated by a certain historical period and have an idea for your own story set in the era? Are your favorite novels historical fiction and you're drawn to create something similar?

What is your heart telling you to write? This is an artist question. Those who write as a business may look at the market to see what is selling and decide to write to the market. There's nothing wrong with that if that motivates you. One thing I've noticed over the years is that markets can be fickle. By the time you write something that is currently selling, readers may be reading something else. That doesn't mean you shouldn't write it, but it does help to be aware.

Although literary trends come and go, there is always room for historical fiction. Some readers are devoted to the genre, which is a good thing for those of us who love to write historical fiction. If there's a historical story tugging at your heartstrings waiting impatiently to be told, then you must write that story.

I often encounter people who have this great idea for a historical novel but haven't found time to write it. I tell them that if the idea isn't pressing them to the point of distraction then it might not be right for them. I tell them that if they have a nice life, a nice job, a nice family, and don't feel a burning desire to write then they probably won't. Thinking you want to write historical fiction and writing historical fiction are not the same thing.

Writing is hard enough when you feel compelled by Fate to do it. It's even harder, if not impossible, when you don't have that burning desire. When is it time to write? When it becomes more painful not to write something than it is to write it. If an idea is gnawing at you and won't leave you to your nice life with your nice family, that's when the writing process begins. When my writing process begins, that's when I flow. Everything else is me pretending to be a normal, well-adjusted person.

Perhaps you feel the same.

DEFINING HISTORICAL FICTION

Writers of historical fiction are not under the same obligation as historians to find evidence for the statements they make. For us it is sufficient if what we say can't be disproved or shown to be false.

~Barry Unsworth

What is historical fiction? There is no one answer to that question since everyone who loves to read or write historical fiction has their own opinions.

However, as the executive editor of a literary journal of historical fiction, I need a clear definition so I know what I'm looking for in the stories my team and I choose to publish. As a writer, I need to know what I'm striving to achieve in my own work.

A few elements of the genre stand out when seeking to define historical fiction. First of all, make sure your story is actually historical in nature, as in it takes place in a clearly defined historical era. This sounds like a no-brainer, right?

You'd be amazed at some of the submissions we receive at *The Copperfield Review.*

We've received many submissions that name a date at the top (1872, for example) but there are no historical facts to help us place the story in that year. Part of the joy of reading historical fiction is learning about the details that could have only come from that era. Typing a year at the top of the first page but not bringing that year to life through vivid information will not endear your story to avid readers of historical fiction. Your story should be clearly historical through events, places, characters, dress, dialogue, and details. Readers should be able to see that you're describing a time other than our own.

Then there are the stories I call memory pieces. Memory pieces are present-day stories with someone having a memory about the past. One character, usually someone older, has a memory from a bygone time but otherwise the story takes place in the present. The editors at *The Copperfield Review* aren't looking to publish memory pieces since the primary story happens in the present.

When do stories have to take place in order to be considered historical fiction? I've read that a story needs to take place at least 50 years ago in order to be considered historical fiction. I've also read that any time period before the author was born could be historical fiction. Rather than focusing on the specific year your story takes place, consider the following questions: Does your story show details specific to that era, showing how things were different between then and now? Does your story share places, events, characters, and dialogue in such a way that we're looking at the time as though it's different from ours?

Having said this, we write fiction to play, experiment, and try things our own way. If you want to write a memory piece, then write a memory piece. Just make sure that the historical segments of the story stand out. Of all my books, it's the *Loving Husband Trilogy*, which goes back and forth between the past and the present, that have been my best sellers. You can tell the difference between the two eras by the language. I don't need to add the date, 1692, for readers to see that now we are in Salem during the witch hunts. The voice, the dialogue, and the descriptions let readers know they have changed centuries.

Tropes in historical fiction can be a little harder to pin down than tropes in other genres. A trope is something commonly seen in any particular format, whether it's books, films, or TV shows, and a trope is used often enough that it becomes recognized as a defining feature of that genre. When we know to expect a duke or an earl in a Regency romance it's because titled heirs have become tropes in that sub-genre.

Tropes for writing historical fiction are fairly basic: placing your story in a believable setting, building a historical world based on research, and using language that feels authentic to the era. We'll talk about each of these features later in the book. There are a few other tropes specific to historical fiction. Many historical novels have characters, usually women, who appear modern in their thinking and actions. Other historical novels are about ordinary people caught up in extraordinary circumstances. Many historical novels have real-life figures who play key roles alongside fictional characters.

From reading submissions for *The Copperfield Review*, it's not particular story tropes I notice as much as time period tropes. There are a lot of historical stories about World War II. Really, a lot. That doesn't mean you shouldn't write about World War II if that's what you want to write, but it does mean you need to work a little harder to make sure your story has something new to offer. At *Copperfield* we also get a lot of stories set in the Old West, Colonial America, and the French Revolution. Again, that doesn't mean these topics are off limits. I've written about Colonial America myself. It simply means that we need to see what our comp novels are (novels by other authors that are comparable to our stories) and figure out what makes our books different.

Quick Write: What is your definition of historical fiction? What do you look for in your favorite historical novels?

As authors, we need to define historical fiction for ourselves. Once you understand what you mean when you say you want to write historical fiction, it becomes easier to bring your story to life because you know what you are trying to accomplish.

4

THE SPARK OF CREATIVITY

I could write historical fiction, or science fiction, or a mystery but since I find it fascinating to research the clues of some little known period and develop a story based on that, I will probably continue to do it.
~Jean M. Auel

Do you know what I mean by "the spark?" It's that germ of creativity, that burst of luminosity that prompts us to say, "I wonder…" after which we spend hours pursuing answers to our questions. The spark of creativity helps us feel or think differently than we did before.

That spark, that moment of wonder, can become a poem, a song, a painting, a film, a dance. It could become a short story or a novel. Sometimes the spark is as fleeting as a lighting flash across a moonless sky and it doesn't become anything other than a passing curiosity. That's okay. Not every spark is destined to become a creative endeavor. But some sparks, after being fed by our imaginations, will grow into something big, bigger than us, even.

How do you know if a spark is merely a passing fancy or something more? Here's what I tell students in my writing classes: if an idea is gnawing at you from the inside out, distracting you to the point where you're unable to think about anything else, then that is probably a spark that will lead to a project of some kind. If the idea tickles your fancy for a day or two but then you aren't interested enough to look into it, then it's simply an idea, maybe even a good idea, but an idea that's not for you. If the question "I wonder…" doesn't inspire more questions, which inspire more questions, then leave this spark aside and find the one that keeps you up at night.

For those of us who are drawn to historical fiction, that "I wonder…" is likely to be motivated by a moment from the past. Creative sparks can come from anywhere—a book you read, a television show, a film, a play, an article in a newspaper, a blog post, a conversation with a friend, a family memory that has been passed down the generations. And creative sparks often come when you least expect them.

In 1994, I saw Ken Burns' documentary about the American Civil War. Like others who have seen the series, I was blown away. I had never seen anything like it. I loved the way the photos from the war were used in the storytelling. I loved how the actors used their voices to portray the emotions of the people who experienced the war. I especially loved the music. I'm embarrassed to admit that I had only a rudimentary knowledge of American history then; I knew what most Americans learn in school—a basic timeline of people and events from the American Revolution on—but this documentary piqued my curiosity.

During one of the documentary episodes it was mentioned that the American Civil War was a war between brothers since for some families the sons fought on opposing sides—one son fought for the Union while another fought for the Confederacy. There, in that one sentence, was my spark of creativity. How could it happen that brothers, brought up in the same house, with the same social mores, would fight on opposing sides of a war? That was the germ for my first historical novel, a story about brothers during the American Civil War.

You never know where your sparks will come from. Jessica is a fellow writer and she stumbled across some information about the 1930s while researching a completely different project. Struck by one spunky young woman's struggle to survive the Great Depression, Jessica decided to write a novel about the young woman's experiences. Wendy is a fashion writer who loves the clothing and the new freedoms found during the Jazz Age so she's writing a novel set in the 1920s. Lin-Manuel Miranda famously read Ron Chernow's biography of Alexander Hamilton, which sparked Miranda's creation of what is arguably one of the most innovative musicals ever (you guessed it), *Hamilton*. One of the great joys of writing historical fiction is that your spark can come from any moment throughout human history. Historical writers can relax knowing there is a vast amount of material to inspire us.

Perhaps your first spark will be inspired by characters— the people who will inhabit your story. Your characters can be fictional or real-life historical personalities. You can choose to create fictional characters who inhabit historical settings such as the Victorian Era or you can focus your writing on real-life people such as Queen Victoria. If you're fascinated by Henry VIII's second wife, the ill-fated Anne Boleyn, you could write about Anne as though she were telling the story, or you could write about Anne from a fictional character's point of view— perhaps a lady in waiting. Philippa Gregory's bestselling *The Other Boleyn Girl* takes a unique look at Anne by comparing and contrasting her experiences with that of her sister, Mary, who had Henry's attention before Anne. Margaret George's *The Autobiography of King Henry VIII: With Notes by His Fool, Will Somers* tells the tale (mostly) from Henry's point of view. Hilary Mantel's Thomas Cromwell Trilogy is a brilliant example of novels based on those closest to Henry VIII. The real-life characters, from King Henry to Anne Boleyn to Thomas Cromwell himself, jump from the page as living, breathing beings.

Do you wonder what Marie Antoinette's life was like, particularly in her final days? Do you wonder what Benjamin Franklin was thinking while he snoozed in his chair at the Constitutional Convention? Do you have a character of your own invention that you imagine wandering the streets of London during the Great Fire of 1666?

My sparks of creativity tend to come from ideas rather than real-life people. Writing about real-life people means that I have to follow the timeline of their lives and I prefer to tell my stories in my own way. That's just me, and the whole point of writing fiction means that you get to do it however you wish.

Perhaps your spark of creativity is inspired by a long-held interest in a specific period. If you're intrigued by Vikings, by the U.S. during the Vietnam War, by cave paintings in France, begin there.

If you're writing a novel set around the French Revolution but don't find the details or the people of the French Revolution particularly interesting, then your novel is already in trouble since you're going to avoid the research with every Excuse you can name. No one wants to study something that bores them. For all the projects I've completed, many more lay by the wayside. If I wasn't compelled by what I was writing, then I dropped it. If I can't convince myself that the project is worth writing, how can I convince a reader that it's worth reading? If you're not interested in your subject, you won't write your novel no matter how much you love the idea of writing historical fiction.

If you're fascinated by the French Revolution, well, that's a different story. Then you'll look forward to digging through the archives, flipping through the bibliographies, and skimming for important details as you search for the next big clue that will help you fit the pieces of your story puzzle together.

When I began writing *Her Dear & Loving Husband*, I was so compelled by the story that I worked on the manuscript nearly every day. I may have taken a Sunday off here and there, but even on those days when I wasn't at the computer the story was on my mind. I wrote the first draft in six weeks. Come to think of it, it was the easiest first draft I've ever written. Why? Because I had to write that story. I couldn't live peacefully with myself if I didn't.

While we're on the subject of sparks of creativity, it might happen that an idea for a historical story occurs to you out of the blue—not based on any previous interest or knowledge but rather some random thought that pops into your mind. You know how those pesky ideas can do that. Then, as a result of the reading that grows out of your curiosity, you develop an interest in the era.

I have this odd habit of coming up with stories set during historical periods I know little or nothing about. In 2009, I came up with an idea for a story set during the Salem Witch Trials in 1692. Though I didn't have any interest in the era before, I became fascinated through my research.

How did I come up with a story idea for an era I wasn't familiar with? It happened when I decided on the setting. As I considered where my paranormal love story would take place, I deliberately stayed away from the Pacific Northwest and

Louisiana since other well-known literary vampires live there. Transylvania was a no-go. I thought of my hometown Los Angeles or where I live now in Las Vegas, but neither felt right. Too bright, I think. I decided that if I wasn't going northwest then how about northeast? I pulled up a map of the U.S., looked at the northeast, saw Massachusetts, and there in a little dot near Boston was Salem. That was it. Once I settled on Salem, I knew I had to incorporate the witch hunts into my story.

When I was writing the second book in the *Loving Husband Series*, I wanted to keep everything readers love about the first book while challenging my characters and myself. I had already used the Salem Witch Trials as the historical background in Book One, and I needed something new to introduce in the sequel. I decided that the Trail of Tears would make a strong historical background for Book Two since the events paralleled the story I wanted to tell.

What did I do with this spark of creativity? I spent most of that summer researching the Trail of Tears, again a time I knew little about. In this case, my spark of creativity gave me an important lens through which to understand the story I wanted to tell.

My creativity has been sparked by various historical periods. I've written about the American Civil War, World War I, the Women's Suffrage Movement, Biblical Jerusalem, the Salem Witch Trials, the Trail of Tears, the Japanese-American internments during World War II, and Victorian England. My next historical fiction project focuses on pioneers on the Oregon Trail. Jump around much? As a matter of fact, I do.

I think my personality causes me to jump from era to era. I'm easily bored, and once I do something I'm ready to move onto a new challenge. What's next? is a frequent question of mine. Yes, I create more work for myself because I have to research a different era for each novel I write, but since I love learning about history I don't mind. Some historical novelists love to write about one specific time period—Ancient Egypt, the American Revolution, World War II. If you're inspired by one historical era, then by all means stick with it. For myself, I'm happy to take my sparks of creativity where I find them. Although I'm taking on extra research, I'm writing the stories that are in my heart to write, which may be one of the biggest gifts you can give yourself as a writer—and one of the biggest gifts you can give your readers because you're sharing your genuine interests with them.

And if the spark turns out to be a fizzle? You have permission to leave behind a project that doesn't suit you. If an idea doesn't work for whatever reason, try another until you find the right fit. Still, don't use this as an excuse to avoid writing. If you want to write historical fiction, you'll need to settle on a project and see it through.

Quick Write: Which historical era do you want to write about? What is it about this era that fascinates you? Do you have ideas for fictional characters or characters based on real-life people? Are there historical figures that have already captured your imagination?

Your answers to these questions will lead you to discover your sparks of creativity, and those sparks will fuel your writing.

5

RESEARCH: DO I HAVE TO?

We've all faced the charge that our novels are history lite, and to some extent, that's true. Yet for some, historical fiction is a way into reading history proper.
~Saul David

Yes. If you want to write historical fiction, you have to research your chosen era. If you don't want to research the history behind your fiction, then writing historical fiction is not for you.

Why would someone want to write historical fiction but not do any research? You'd be amazed. I hear from writers who want to write their great tome—the greatest historical novel yet written—and still they avoid research with the X, Y, Zs of Excuses. When I'm discussing story ideas with prospective historical novelists, often I'll ask them where they are in their research.

"Research…?"

I can feel the pause between the lines in their emails.

"Well," they say, "I've had to (insert favorite Excuse here): _____."

My personal go-to Excuse is "I had to have a serious conversation with Poppy (my cat) about... ." Most of my Excuses have to do with my cat. What that says about me, I don't know.

Here's a secret about writing historical fiction that we don't often hear: research can be fun. I promise. I'm not high, I don't drink, and I am, as far as I know, sane. If you develop a genuine passion for a certain time in history, you'll look forward to your research. If you're prompted to write historical fiction because of a lifelong interest in World War I, for example, chances are you've been doing research all along. If you're first learning about your era, or learning more so you can write your story with depth and detail, you can still find great enjoyment in the research process.

Whether you have chosen your historical era from a random idea, a life-long interest in a certain period, or you develop a fascination for the history from your research, you need to enjoy the time spent in your historical era. You're going to be there awhile. And don't forget, it's not only your interest in the history that has to be piqued—it's your readers' interest as well. If you're dragging your heels when it's time to research, imagine how your readers will feel when they read your story.

I'm a big believer in the power of energy. I've always felt that the writer's enthusiasm, or lack thereof, can be felt by the reader. Have you ever read a novel that felt bland, as though every blah the author ever felt was there for everyone to read? The opposite is also true. I've read novels where energy leaps from the page. These are the books that keep me reading late into the night because I can't wait until morning to get back to that world. It's more than the storyline or the characters or the writing style that makes some stories pop while others put us quietly to sleep. The writer's enthusiasm can make the difference between a story that sings and a story that struggles.

Of course, we need to craft our stories to the best of our abilities. But beyond raw craft lies the connection we feel as writers to the worlds we are creating. If you're writing about a period of history that doesn't suit you for whatever reason, readers will sense it. If you're struggling to find something interesting through your research, readers will know. Finding a period in history we genuinely want to learn about is the first hoop we have to jump through when we begin writing historical fiction.

6

WHITTLING DOWN

As a writer of historical fiction, I believe you don't want to fictionalize gratuitously; you want the fictional aspects to prod and pressure the history into new and exciting reactions.
~Matthew Pearl

After you've chosen your time period, or after your time period has chosen you (as it occasionally happens), the first thing you need to do is narrow your topic to a workable size. This is particularly true if you're dealing with a vast subject like the American Civil War. To research the entire war would be too huge of a project, that is unless you were Shelby Foote and willing to dedicate 20 years of your life to the task as he did. There is simply too much material to shift through. Think of it this way: the historical period is the frame through which we observe our characters in action. The frame helps us decide which specific details we'll need to tell our stories.

Michelangelo said, "Every block of stone has a statue inside it and it is the task of the sculptor to discover it." Just as a block of stone can have a statue inside, a daydream can contain a story. We, the writers, must whittle away to discover those stories. We have to work at our ideas to find the narrative that is there, waiting to be told.

When you narrow down your topic, your research becomes less burdensome. One way to whittle down your topic is to narrow your historical focus. You might focus on the life of a particular individual, but even then you have to decide which aspects of the person's life to illuminate. You might also limit your focus to something like a single event, a single year, or a single battle. When I researched my American Civil War story, I kept my focus on one regiment during the final year of the war. That's still a sizable topic because a lot happened the last year of the war, but the fact that I was concentrating on a single regiment helped me stay focused.

It's easy to be distracted by the abundance of information out there. Some writers call it the "rabbit hole of research." This looks interesting, and that's cool, and "Ooh! There's a squirrel!" There's nothing wrong with reading interesting tidbits here and there; in fact, sometimes those tidbits lead to substantial breakthroughs that will help you connect the dots of your story. I experience the "Ooh! There's a squirrel!" syndrome on a daily basis when I'm researching, so I understand perfectly well how dizzying the process can be. The trick is to have a plan before you begin. This is what I'm researching. This is what I'm looking for. True, you want to read around your era in a general way for your own knowledge, but when you're looking for the facts that will make your story pop off the page, the more specific you can be the better.

Sometimes we're lucky and we know immediately what we want to research. We're familiar with the era, we know exactly where we want to focus, and the research moves forward seamlessly. Other times, it can be hard to narrow our topic, especially if we're not yet sure what years or events our stories will cover. That happened to me when I was researching *Victory Garden*.

When I began *Victory Garden*, all I had was a vague idea that I wanted to explore the fight for American women's voting rights. I had been watching a news show where they discussed the apathy of American voters, and for some reason my overactive brain recalled when I was in the fifth grade and my class read a story about a woman who was arrested for demanding the right to vote. I can't remember the name of the story, but I remember that she was kept in a squalid cell and force-fed because she refused to eat while she was in prison. I hadn't thought of that story since fifth grade, but suddenly I wondered what that experience must have been like. Who was that woman? How did she get there? After kicking the idea around a bit, I realized there was a story in there I wanted to explore.

How did I whittle through the excess to find the kernel of the story? First, I did some general research to get a sense of the era. By general research I mean I read books and articles about American women fighting for the right to vote. I wasn't looking for anything specific because I didn't know enough to be specific. I wanted an idea of what the American women's suffrage movement looked like since I knew next to nothing about it.

As I gained knowledge about the *what* of the era, I began to see a *who*—a young woman living through the events of the American women's suffrage movement. I knew she was riled up by how women were treated as second-class citizens. I knew she made the decision to be part of the solution, which meant fighting for the vote. I saw her go to Washington, DC to picket the White House. She too would be arrested and she too would be force-fed.

Once my story had a direction I was able to focus on more specific aspects of the American women's suffrage movement. What brought the women to Washington, DC? Why did they picket? Why were they arrested and force-fed? Here's some American history trivia: did you know that there were many American women *against* the women's suffrage movement? A surprising number of women believed that women didn't have the stamina for something as strenuous as forming political opinions and voting. The irony, of course, is that the anti-suffrage women campaigned as hard as their pro-suffrage counterparts, thereby doing exactly what they claimed women couldn't do. Who were these women working against their own right to vote? The anti-suffrage movement added another layer of interest to my story. I also discovered that the final phase of the women's suffrage movement coincided with American participation in World War I and the war had an important impact on the women's quest for votes.

I decided that the story would take place between 1917 and 1920, when women received the vote. Finally, I saw my fictional character moving through these real-life events, participating in the suffrage movement, watching friends come home from the war, and caring for family infected with the deadly flu during the 1918 pandemic. Yeah, I know.

Another inspiration, gleaned from my research, came from my discovery that moving pictures and vaudeville were popular entertainments then. For your reading entertainment, here's an example of my brain making connections between two unalike things, which happens frequently when I'm writing fiction. My uncle Bruce Arenstein was a huge fan of the old-time vaudeville comedians—Laurel and Hardy, the Three Stooges, W.C. Fields, and Abbott and Costello. My favorites have always been the Marx Brothers. After Uncle Bruce passed, I brought home some of his books, one of which was written by Harpo Marx about his life on the vaudeville circuit with his brothers. Suddenly, my character, Rose, had a love interest, a vaudeville actor who, you guessed it, travels the country in a musical comedy act with his brothers. Thanks, Uncle Bruce.

I had several aspects to address in *Victory Garden* (the women's suffrage movement, World War I, the flu pandemic, and vaudeville), but because I knew exactly what I wanted to cover it was easier for me to find the information I needed.

Consider your own story ideas. Perhaps by this point you have a general sense of what you want to write about: Biblical Jerusalem, Paris during the Jazz Age, medieval English peasants perhaps? Can you narrow your topic to a workable size? Do you know what area or events you want to focus on?

Quick Write:

1. What is your general topic? (This can be broad, like the American Revolution or the life of Henry VIII.)

2. How will you narrow your topic to a workable size? (Hint: if you aren't yet able to dig deep into your topic, do some general reading about the era. Don't look for anything specific. You're reading to get a sense of the time, that's all.)

3. Once you're able to narrow your topic, what will be the focus of your research?

Here you should be more specific: I'm writing about the last year of Abraham Lincoln's life. I'm writing about the first battle of the Korean War. If your topic is still too broad, don't worry. You can always whittle it down more later. In fact, as it often happens, you may come up with such good ideas from your research that you completely change your vision for your story. Don't be afraid to revise your original ideas. Revising means you're thinking deeply and being honest about what will make your story the best it can be.

The task of digging through mountains of information can seem daunting. But if you can narrow your topic to a workable size, then you're making your research time purposeful and even enjoyable. Or am I the only one who likes weeding through historical information and taking notes. Anyone? Anyone?

7

WHAT KIND OF INFORMATION DO I NEED?

Concentrate your narrative energy on the point of change. This is especially important for historical fiction. When your character is new to a place, or things alter around them, that's the point to step back and fill in the details of their world.
~Hilary Mantel

When we're writing historical fiction we're wearing two hats at the same time—the hat that we wear as novelists where we utilize plot, characterization, and point of view (I always picture this as a tall, red and white striped Cat in the Hat hat) and the hat we wear as armchair historians where we weed through details of the past to find those gems that will make our stories sparkle (I picture this as a professor-style bowler hat). No matter what I'm writing, in whatever era, there are certain details I always look for in my research.

You want to carry your readers into your world by touching their senses. Your readers should feel as though they are standing alongside your characters in that place and time.

What do they see, hear, taste, touch, and smell? Often it's the smaller details, what people wore, what they ate, the houses they lived in, that brings historical fiction alive since these are details we can relate to, even if what we eat and drink and where we live is different today. Remember, historical novelists are world builders as much as fantasy writers, only our worlds are based on places and people that once existed.

1. Clothing

Studying what people wore during your time period can be a lot of fun. Pinterest is perfect for this since you can often find examples of the clothing you want to describe. I like seeing how fashions have changed over the years, and I have a particular appreciation for the fact that as a twenty-first century woman I don't have to wear corsets or stays. I like breathing, thank you very much. Ruth Goodman, in her book *How to Be a Victorian: A Dawn-to-Dusk Guide to Victorian Life*, describes what it's like to wear Victorian clothing and undergarments. When I was writing *When It Rained at Hembry Castle*, my sweet Victorian romance, and I was describing Daphne's bustle, all I could think was, "Thank God I don't have to wear that!"

YouTube is also a great place to find examples of clothing from various eras. There are many videos showing historical clothing, how it was made, and how it was worn. I found a great video of a woman dressing for an 1870s ball on YouTube while writing *Hembry*.

You don't want to go overboard describing clothing since that could distract from your story. Whatever details you share, you want those details to flow seamlessly through the narrative. Don't stop to describe an outfit in minute detail, that is unless the outfit plays some larger role in that scene or that story. There has to be a reason why you're bringing these specific details to the reader's attention. Does someone see a woman in her stays who shouldn't? That would be a reason to describe those stays.

We're telling stories set during an era we don't live in, so we can't assume that our readers know what people wore in seventeenth-century Massachusetts, or any other time period. We don't want to spend two paragraphs describing clothing since that would slow down the action, but we do need a few details to help immerse readers in the time.

2. Hairstyles

Treat hairstyles the same way you treat clothing. Unless your novel has a specific reason to dwell on Marie Antoinette's ship-shaped wig, you don't want to spend a lot of time describing hairstyles. Use a gentle touch. Again, a few deftly shared details can help your reader visualize your characters.

3. Food

I think I missed my calling in this life. I should have been a food historian. I love researching and describing the food of the era I'm writing about. Sometimes, in true food historian form, I'll even cook a few historically accurate recipes. I love to cook, so exploring historical recipes is something I enjoy. You don't need to go to such lengths by any means. My habit of including meals in my fiction is largely influenced by my love of Dickens, who delighted in describing food. I do think readers are more interested in reading about food than other details because what people ate gives a particular insight into the era, and, hey, who doesn't like food?

Studying the foods of Biblical Jerusalem while writing *Woman of Stones* was fascinating since food plays such an important role in the story. Here's an example of the cool things you learn when you study food. During the era of the Second Temple (from 516 BCE to 70 CE) bread was the staple food. Garlic, coriander, cumin, and oregano were used as seasonings, all of which are still commonly used today, along with walnuts and persimmon. I found recipes for challah (braided bread) and cholent (a hearty slow-cooked beef stew) that I made myself. Yes, I use modern appliances, though food historians will only use materials available during the time they are studying. The point, for me at least, is not to recreate the way they actually cooked but to taste the flavors and smell the aromas.

Breaking bread brings a sense of community in a profound way, and sharing our characters' meals allows us another way to show how our characters interact with each other. When I researched *When It Rained at Hembry Castle*, I found *Mrs. Beeton's Book of Household Management*, first published in 1861, which contains some of the most popular dishes of the Victorian era. Discovering recipes for gravies, puddings, and pies, as well as main courses, helped my *Hembry* friends eat well. As they're sharing a delicious meal we can join them at the table and listen in on their conversations and learn who they are and how they fit into their world.

4. Conflicts

There is no story without conflict, and you never want to make things too easy for your characters. When things are too easy there's nothing for your characters, or your readers, to hope for. If you're writing historical fiction, you may find that the conflicts of the era provide the challenges your characters must overcome. The fact that women didn't have the vote provided the main conflict for *Victory Garden*, and the Salem witch hunts were the conflict for *Her Dear & Loving Husband* and *Down Salem Way*. We'll talk more about conflict in a later chapter since conflict is central to storytelling.

5. People

Who were the real-life people important to your era? How will your fictional characters interact with these real-life people? How can real-life people add interest to your story? Perhaps your story will even be centered on a real-life historical figure. No matter how you choose to include real-life figures, you need to know who the important people from your era are and you should understand their role in history.

6. Buildings and Places

What is the geography of the place you're writing about? Where do your characters live? What do your characters' homes look like based on the era and their social status? The stately home in *When It Rained at Hembry Castle* plays an important role in the story. I even named the novel after it. James Wentworth's home, a seventeenth-century wooden house built before the Salem witch hunts, proves to be an important character in *Her Dear & Loving Husband*.

As with other historical details, the best time to bring attention to buildings and places is when your character notices those places. Is this the house where your characters live? If so, then they would notice the creaking stairs. Are your characters on a journey and discovering new places? Then they would notice new sights and sounds.

7. Culture

I love learning about the culture of the era I'm writing about. In addition to learning about the food and the places, I love discovering what people read, how they spent their free time, the art they looked at, the music they listened to, and their lifestyles in general. Touches of culture can add a deeper layer of interest to our stories.

GRAPES

One trick I learned from a history class I took years ago is to think about the historical world I'm creating through the acronym GRAPES. All societies have them—GRAPES, I mean, though they might have grapes too.

Geography—How does the climate and landscape affect the people who live there?

Religion—How does the society's belief system and traditions affect the people who live there?

Achievements—What are the achievements of this society—good and bad?

Politics—What is the power structure in this society?

Economics—How are goods and resources used in this society?

Social Structure—How does this society organize people into classes? Who ends up in which class and why?

There are several ways you can weave historical details through your fiction. You can share the details in dialogue, the story's narration, or your characters' thoughts. No matter how you share your historical details, remember that we don't want to burden our readers with an information dump. If we do as Hilary Mantel suggests and focus on points of change, where our characters notice new things, then we have a logical place to step back and fill in the information that makes historical fiction special.

Quick Write:

What types of information do you think you will need for your historical story? What bits and pieces will add layers of interest to your characters and their lives? You may need to come back to these questions after you've done some initial research.

8

CONSIDER YOUR SOURCES

One of the joys of writing historical fiction is the chance to read as much as you like on a pet subject—so much that you could easily bore your friends senseless on the topic.
~Deanna Raybourn

By this point, you may have some sense of the information you'll need to breathe life into the historical world you are creating. The information you need may change as you get to know your story better, and that's okay. You need to start somewhere, so start with the basics. One of the keys to writing historical fiction, or any fiction, is flexibility. You begin with some ideas, you learn new things, and then your ideas change and grow and you realize you need to learn different things. An author with a flexible mind is an author open to possibilities.

In order to find the information you are going to need, you should consider your sources. Let's take a moment to understand the differences between primary, secondary, and tertiary sources. All are valuable to historical novelists.

Primary Sources

Primary sources are documents from people who were alive during that time in history. If you are writing a historical novel about George Washington, you're in luck since he left behind a wealth of letters and diaries. A primary source can be any type of artifact left behind by those who were there— diaries, documents, books, letters, articles, speeches, memoirs, and autobiographies. If you are studying a later time in history, then primary sources might include photographs, recordings, or films. If you can get your hands on primary sources then do because it makes a world of difference when you can learn from those who were there. Primary sources allow you to hear authentic voices from the past without needing a fairground gypsy to act as a conduit.

When I was researching *Victory Garden*, I spent hours at my university library reading newspaper clippings from the early twentieth century. I focused on papers from 1917 through 1920, the years my novel takes place. I was fascinated by the derogatory tone towards the women's suffrage move-ment in the *New York Times*. The advertisements were also interesting to my modern eyes. On the surface, everything appears so innocent—the Coca-Cola ads featuring Gibson Girls in their striped dresses, the blemish cream ads, the shaving cream ads. Next to the ads were scathing editorials against women fighting for the vote. I wouldn't have noticed that contrast if I hadn't read those copies of the *New York Times*.

When you read a letter written by someone who sat down to dinner with George Washington and experienced the man first hand, you get a clearer idea of Washington (at least from the recorder's point of view). A letter written by Washington himself might add even more clarity to his character (at least from his point of view), which is what we seek to do when writing historical fiction—create clarity of character. We need to paint believable pictures of the people who inhabit our historical worlds.

The more primary sources you can find, the deeper your understanding will be. After all, we can't help our readers know an era if we don't know it ourselves. It takes more effort to discover primary sources, but it's worth the time. Not all primary sources are easy to access, and some time periods, especially if they are far enough in the past, may not have primary sources. Still, I recommend searching to see what's out there. You may be surprised. Primary sources put a finger on the pulse of the times in a way little else can. What were people thinking and feeling then? As writers of historical fiction, it's our job to find out, and primary sources can help.

Secondary Sources

Secondary sources are written by people who did not experience that time for themselves. Biographies, nonfiction accounts of a historical era, and scholarly articles are examples of secondary sources.

Often, secondary sources offer analysis or interpretation of primary sources. For example, if you're reading biographies about George Washington, Washington's biographers have combed through primary sources and developed a character portrait. Reading Ron Chernow's *Washington: A Life* is a great way to do some general reading about the first American president. If I were writing a historical novel about Washington, I would read Washington's letters for myself, as well as the letters of those who knew him, and I would read as many biographies as I could get my hands on. That doesn't mean that the biographers have the final word in how I interpret George Washington. As much as I respect the biographers' interpretations, I want to make my own decisions since I'm the one writing the novel. If I don't develop my own sense of who this guy Washington was, then my novel will be in trouble because I won't have a personal connection to my subject. Research allows me to decide what I think about George Washington, not what the biographers think about George Washington. By the way, I have no intention of writing a novel about George Washington, so if you like the idea it's yours.

Secondary sources are the most easily accessible, so look for books by historians, biographers, and social critics.

Tertiary Sources

Tertiary sources are a combination of primary and secondary sources. Tertiary sources provide a summary of information in the form of a database, an encyclopedia, or a bibliography. One trick I learned while pursuing my Ph.D. (which is essentially a research degree) is to find a book or article that matches the topic I'm writing about and then scan the bibliography (a tertiary source) to find other books or articles on the same topic. Scanning bibliographies saves time since I'm starting with a list of books and articles that cover the information I'm looking for. Trust me. It works.

Using the internet

Wikipedia articles are tempting since they are often the first articles to pop up on our screens when we're searching for information online. Wiki is a cute name, but the mistakes in some of the articles aren't so cute. As historical novelists, we need to resist the temptation to give into easy. We need to dig deeper, as in maybe scroll past the first or second suggestion in our web search. I'm not saying Wikipedia is all bad, and often, if I can't resist the temptation and my finger clicks on the Wikipedia entry before I know what I'm doing, I'll scroll down to the articles to see where the information comes from. Then I'll click on those articles and read them to determine if the information comes from a reputable source.

I've found a lot of accurate information on the internet, and there's no reason to assume all sites are fraudulent. When using the internet, however, be aware that there will be gaps in the research since internet articles are often on the short side and may lack the depth you would find in books and journals.

I once took a technology class where the instructor showed us how to make judgments about where internet information comes from. Generally speaking, .edu sources are the most reliable since the information comes from a university. The Washington Papers are curated by the University of Virginia's George Washington scholars. Next in line would be the .gov and .org websites. Try to avoid .net and .com sites when you can. The problem with a .net or a .com website is anyone can have one. This doesn't mean the information is necessarily bad, and I have found sound information on .com sites when the writer added links to show where the information came from. Still, some personal websites may share the opinion of the website owner as opposed to presenting the scholarly work you would expect from a .edu site. Some people share their opinions as if they are facts. I'm not ·naming names.

True, most of us can spot an opinion-based website, but it helps to stay aware. My rule of thumb is that if I find information on the internet I want to use in my research, I check the original source of the information and then double check that against at least two other sources. If I see the same information in two or three other places, I have the confidence that either a.) the information is correct, or b.) everyone is making the same mistake, which makes my mistake less noticeable.

Two internet tools I refer to again and again are Google Scholar (scholar.google.com) and Google Books (books.-google.com). Scholarly articles can cost up to $30 a pop depending on the publisher, but you can find some free-to-download pdfs on Google Scholar. Articles on Google Scholar tend to be written for academics, but if you have the patience to weed through the subject-related jargon you might find some well-researched, peer-reviewed information about your historical era. I've also found great information through Google Books. Some older editions on Google Books are available to read for free, but even if there is only a chapter or two available I can often glean some helpful knowledge from there. If I find the book particularly helpful I often purchase it since it's something I'd like to have in my research library.

Other dependable research sites I've used are Project Gutenberg (http://www.gutenberg.org/), the Library of Congress (https://www.loc.gov/collections/), the Victorian Web (http://victorianweb.org/), V&A (https://collections.-vam.ac.uk/), and JSTOR (https://www.jstor.org/). The History Quill has a list of 50+ research sites for writers of historical fiction. You can find it here: https://thehistoryquill.com/50-plus-top-online-research-resources-for-historical-fiction-writers/. Here is the link to the Washington Papers for those of you who want to write about George: https://washingtonpapers.org/.

The internet is great for finding interesting snippets. When I was researching Victorian England, I stumbled on a scholarly site that explains the Victorian languages of flowers and fans. Even the way a Victorian woman held her fan could send a message to a nearby gentleman. I used the fan with fun effect in a ballroom scene where a young lady sends a discreet signal to her favorite gentleman.

The internet becomes a truly wonderful research tool, though, when you're in the middle of writing a scene and realize you're missing some important fact in your notes. When I was writing *Her Dear & Loving Husband* I had the task of writing scenes set on a college campus I hadn't visited. I needed to know where one building was in relation to another and how far someone had to walk to get from one place to the other. I did a quick internet search, printed up a map of the campus, and I was able to write my scene in a realistic way. While that part of the story isn't particularly historical (it's a present-day college in the present-day town of Salem, Massachusetts), my point still stands.

Is the Source Sound?

Historians use two factors to decide whether or not a source appears to be sound—authenticity and authority. Does the source appear authentic and therefore credible? What authority does the person have who is making these claims? Is the authority a university professor who spends her life studying that topic? Or is it Joe Schmo saying whatever comes to mind? Is the information verifiable? Is there more than one source so we can cross-reference?

As historical novelists we don't necessarily need to go to such lengths when considering our sources. After all, we aren't historians. But we should at least consider these questions when deciding which sources seem authentic and authoritative and which should be left aside.

Your Assignment:

Now it's time to start locating sources. Find two primary sources and two secondary sources for your research. You should also find two tertiary sources such as bibliographies since more than likely the bibliographies will serve as the springboard for the rest of your information search. Once you start locating sources, you'll find more sources, and more sources, until research becomes a thunderous waterfall raining on your head. If you start to feel overwhelmed by the sheer amount of information, then by all means stop searching and start reading what you have.

At the same time, don't shy away from the vast resources at your disposal. The more information you have to work with the better. As researchers, it's always better to work from wealth than poverty. You can leave aside information you don't need but you can't create a believable historical world from a dearth of details. Read as much as you can without babbling about what you learned to your cat. Maybe that's just me. Read so much that you're boring your friends with what you learn, as Deanna Raybourn says.

Even if most of the information doesn't end up in your novel (and most of it won't), it's still knowledge that will act as the backbone for the information you do share. Everything you learn will inform your writing, and the more of an expert you become, the more expertly you can carry your readers into your chosen era.

As writers of historical fiction, it's our job to paint the scenes of our stories with details. We discover those details through our research.

9

TAKE NOTES AND THEN MORE NOTES...

I went to grad school with the grand plan of getting my Ph.D. and writing weighty, Tudor-Stuart-set historical fiction - from which I emerged with a law degree and a series of light-hearted historical romances about flower-named spies during the Napoleonic wars.
~Lauren Willig

I'm with Lauren. I got my Ph.D. with the intention of becoming a university professor and instead I write and edit historical fiction.

After I've read as much about my subject as my brain can handle, I'll begin to form ideas about how I can incorporate the history into the fiction I want to write. That's when I begin to take notes.

Some writers prefer to type their notes or write them on index cards. One writer friend of mine posts his research notecards on a bulletin board by his desk. His board is divided into sections, one section for each chapter in his book, and he pins his notecards into the chapter where he thinks the information will go.

Although I've gone digital to a large degree, there are still times when I prefer to handwrite my notes into a spiral notebook. In *Writing Down the Bones*, Natalie Goldberg recommends getting notebooks with cartoon characters on the covers because it prevents you from taking yourself too seriously while you're writing, which is a great idea, especially at this early stage of the process where anything and everything about your story is likely to change and nothing should be taken too seriously.

Writing notes the old-fashioned way, with pen and paper, can seem like a tedious chore to some, but, like Goldberg, I believe there's a hand to heart connection in writing things out longhand. I won't bore you with the details, but there are studies that say that we tend to learn better if we handwrite something as opposed to typing it or copying and pasting. If you really want to learn the information then you might consider taking notes with pen and paper.

When I take the time to handwrite my notes I absorb the information in a deeper way. Since I understand the information better, the historical details flow through my story more naturally than they would if I had mindlessly copied and pasted my research. When I take the short cut and copy and paste, I skim and find only what I think I need and ignore the rest. When I handwrite my notes I'm forced to slow down, read carefully, and decide what is important enough to write down. Since it's a slower process I have time to think. Thinking is a good thing, especially when crafting a story.

That isn't to say you must read every single word in the books and articles you're using for research. Scholarly articles begin with abstracts (a thumbnail summary of the article), so if a scholarly article has caught your interest then read the abstract first. If you like the abstract, then read the introduction. If the article wasn't written for a peer-reviewed journal, then it may start with the introduction. Either way, after you read the abstract and/or the introduction and you still think the material is a good fit, read the conclusion. If you're still interested, read the parts in between. If a section doesn't match your area of research, or if it doesn't give you any new information or insights, skip it.

When it comes to books, start with the table of contents. Does the book cover topics you're interested in? From there, visit the index to find the page numbers for the specific information you need. You don't want to waste valuable research time, but if something catches your attention then by all means read more about it. Great ideas can come from interesting tidbits we weren't specifically looking for. It's okay to skim to find what you're looking for, but don't skim so much that you gloss over some potentially useful information.

Part of becoming comfortable with the research process is figuring out what works for you. The notes, in whatever form you write them, come in handy after the library books have been returned and you need that certain date while you're working. And don't forget to write down the bibliographical information for each source (the author, title of the work, publication date, publisher, and the page number where you found the information or the website address). You may need those sources again. It has happened to me where I returned a book to the library or deleted an article from my file and then realized I needed more information. Keeping a working bibliography is time well spent.

10

MAKE FRIENDS WITH A LIBRARIAN (AND ANYONE ELSE WHO KNOWS YOUR SUBJECT)

I can read a newspaper article, and it might trigger something else in my mind. I often like to choose in historical fiction things or subject matter I don't feel have been given a fair shake in history.
~Kathryn Lasky

I've already admitted my love for the instant gratification of finding some necessary information online in a matter of moments. However, nothing replaces library research. Some writers may be intimidated by the sheer amount of resources in the library, but never fear.

I've encountered many conscientious librarians who have helped me track down an elusive book or article about a little-known subject. If you're not sure where to begin your quest for knowledge about your historical period, ask a librarian. Most are more than happy to help. And I'm not just saying that because my character Sarah Wentworth from the *Loving Husband Trilogy* is a librarian. I've always had a high opinion of librarians (as most book lovers do), and I've thought more than once that if I weren't doing what I'm doing, or a being a food historian, I'd be a librarian.

If your local library doesn't have what you're looking for, most library systems have a program where, if a local branch doesn't have a book you want but another branch does, the other branch will ship the book to your neck of the woods so you don't have to run all over town. Check with your local library to see if it has a similar program.

In the digital age we no longer have to hover over clunky wooden catalogs and pull out musty cards that leave us grabbing for our asthma inhalers. These days, libraries have online catalogs, and often I'll check the catalog at home before I head into the library to see if they have what I need. I've even checked out books at home and had them waiting for me at the circulation desk when I arrived.

Coming from the academic world, I highly recommend visiting a university library. After all, university libraries are created for research. University libraries have online databases that make it possible to discover information you might not find otherwise, and yes, you can access them from your home computer if you're a member of that library. Some university libraries still have newspapers, journals, microfiche, and other hard to find materials, though most of it is digital now. Other university libraries have primary sources in their special collections. Sometimes these special collections are only available to scholars, but sometimes they aren't. Some university libraries are open to the public for a yearly fee, and if you can afford the fee then it can be a worthwhile investment. Whether you're a member of the university library or not, you can still access their onsite resources. You won't be able to check anything out, but you can bring pen and paper to take notes or your credit card and make copies.

I know I'm stating the obvious when I mention using the

library, but sometimes I feel like I need to remind people that there are these buildings with wall to wall books you can borrow for free. That's the books you can borrow for free, not the buildings. With so many people using the internet as their only source of research, I worry that they are passing over other important avenues to information.

Finally, don't be afraid to reach out to historians, professors, or anyone else who might be knowledgeable about your topic. If you're looking to speak to a historian who has written a book you're using for research, often an author's contact information can be found in their books or on their websites and you can email the expert directly. Be respectful of their time and don't ask for lengthy explanations on difficult subjects. A quick answer to your polite question is all you're looking for. Some experts will answer your queries. Some won't. Some might even agree to a brief face to face interview if you're in the area.

Maybe the expert is closer to home. Maybe the expert is someone who knows what plants were used for healing purposes during your era. Maybe the expert is someone who has been where your characters live and they can give you insight into the area. Maybe the expert is your own family member who might have information you need. There are experts on many subjects all around you. Tap into their knowledge.

11

RESEARCHING HISTORICAL FICTION: SOME IDEAS

What really disconcerts commentators, I suspect, is that when they read historical fiction, they feel their own lack of education may be exposed; they panic, because they don't know which bits are true.
~Hilary Mantel

The way I research historical fiction has changed a lot over the years. When I first started writing historical fiction, I would check as many books as I could carry out of the library, take meticulous notes, color code my notes with high-lighters (blue for food, pink for fashion, etc.), return those books and check out another pile, and so on until I felt I had enough knowledge to begin drafting my story. Sometimes it was months worth of research before I started writing anything. Once I started writing I knew exactly where to look in my notebook for what I needed. If I was writing a dinner scene, I could find my notes about food. Notes I referred to often, such as important dates or events that I kept mentioning, were written on index cards, also color-coded, for easier access.

I no longer complete my research before I start writing. As a fellow writer friend said to me, feeling like you have to do all of your research before you start writing slows down your process to the point where your story doesn't get written. These days I do some preliminary research by reading generally around my topic, perhaps taking a few notes, just enough to keep things clear in my head, and then I begin the prewriting process. Usually, through the process of brainstorming, prewriting, and drafting my story, I recognize what specific bits of historical information I'll need and then I'll search for those bits. That's when my note taking begins in earnest. I create digital folders to organize my notes, citations, and annotations, and I still keep categories of information together (food, clothing, political climate, and so on).

Just like the writing process, the research process must be your own. Try spiral notebooks with different colored pens. Try a different notebook for different areas of your research. Color code your notes with highlighters like I used to. If you're completely digital then you can use a program like Scrivener where you can create different files within your novel folder. You can also create different Google docs or Word files for each area of research. You can do all your research up front like I used to, or you can do it piecemeal as I do now. Just as there is no one way to write, there is no one way to research. Experiment with your research process. Try something new. See if it works for you. If not, no worries, try something else.

It's worth repeating that not everything I learn through my research will end up in my story. It's worth repeating because I've read more than one historical novel where suddenly there's an information dump, as if the author had to incorporate every piece of research into the book or else. The problem, though, is that information dumps are boring because they slow the action down, which we never want to do.

Sometimes unused research ends up in another book. That's especially true if you write different novels set during the same era. I did a lot of research into the Salem Witch Trials when I wrote *Her Dear & Loving Husband*. Since the novel moves back and forth between present-day Salem and Salem in 1692, I didn't use all my research. There wasn't room for it in that narrative arc. However, when I wrote *Down Salem Way*, the prequel to *Her Dear & Loving Husband*, I was able to incorporate a lot of that unused research.

If you're writing historical fiction based on a long-held interest in a certain time period, then congratulations! You already have an excellent overview of that era. *When It Rained at Hembry Castle* was the first historical novel I wrote based on a time period I was already familiar with.

For my Master's degree in English I studied Victorian literature and my thesis was about Dickens. I came up with the original idea for *Hembry Castle* 20 years ago (no joke) when I decided I wanted to write a story set in Victorian England about a writer who would be loosely based on a young Charles Dickens. I wrote other novels and kept the Victorian story on the back burner. After I fell in love with *Downton Abbey*, I realized that I could take elements from that TV show and use it to bring my Victorian story to life.

When it came time to research *Hembry Castle*, I began with the author I know best—you guessed it—Dickens. I've read all his novels, many more than once, most more than twice. I started with the Dickens novel I knew had the most in common with the story I had in mind for *Hembry—Our Mutual Friend*. From there, I returned to a few favorite nonfiction books about the Victorian era. I discovered a new favorite historian, Ruth Goodman, who impressed me with the fact that she doesn't just talk about Victorian clothing, she makes it and wears it. Goodman has tried out many elements of living in the Victorian era. Her book, *How To Be a Victorian: A Dawn-to-Dusk Guide to Victorian Life*, is a must-read for anyone interested in the Victorian period. Edward Ellis is the character based on a young Dickens, but I didn't need to read anything specifically for that since I had already read pretty much every biography about Dickens. It was nice to be able to use information I had in my head for a change.

As I stumbled through my first draft of *Hembry*, I gained a clearer sense of what information I needed to bring that story to life. I realized that if Edward is a political journalist (like Dickens in his early career) then he would know politics. That seems obvious, I know, but I'm a little slow sometimes. When I began researching the political climate I knew specifically what I was looking for—events in English politics in 1870. I remembered a class I had taken about Victorian England, and one of the topics covered was Gladstone and Disraeli. I read about them to refresh my memory, and though I didn't use much of the political information in the novel, it provided me with useful background knowledge.

Victorians were governed by specific rules for every aspect of their lives, and since part of Daphne's Meriwether's struggle in *Hembry* is learning to live in her father's rigid world, she has to learn those rules. I found *The Essential Handbook of Victorian Etiquette* by Thomas E. Hill and I used Hill's book as one of my references for Victorian etiquette. I had a lot of fun writing the scenes where manners take center stage since Daphne is rather amused by her grandmother's nitpicking about how Daphne is not refined enough for Society.

It's a great feeling when I can start to see how I can weave the history into the story I want to tell. That weaving is a kind of storytelling magic that can only happen as a result of research.

TRAVELING FOR RESEARCH

The thing that most attracts me to historical fiction is taking the factual record as far as it is known, using that as scaffolding, and then letting imagination build the structure that fills in those things we can never find out for sure.

~Geraldine Brooks

You don't need to travel to the place you're writing about, but it can be helpful to go if you can. If you're writing about Boston during the American Revolution, it adds depth to your descriptions if you're able to walk the Freedom Trail for yourself. If you're writing about France or Hawaii or Israel, and you have the time and the budget, there's nothing better than standing on the ground you're writing about. There's something visceral about walking the walks, hearing the sounds, seeing the sights, and experiencing the local lifestyle. Eating the food is good too. Obviously, being there in the twenty-first century won't be the same as being there during whatever century you're writing about; still, it can be meaningful to simply *be there*. Visiting the location may also give you a chance to visit museums and libraries that you wouldn't have access to otherwise.

Sometimes during travel you discover a jewel you didn't know you were looking for. That happened to me when I was in Portland, Oregon and found my way to Pittock Mansion, nestled in the West Hills with a panoramic view of the city below. At the time, I was doing my initial research for *When It Rained at Hembry Castle*. When I was visiting Portland I saw an advertisement for Pittock Mansion and knew I had to visit since it sounded like a stately home similar to the one I was writing about in *Hembry*.

That afternoon I stood in an old home that echoes the grand English country house in *Downton Abbey*, at least as much as a frontier American house can. I had assumed that Highclere Castle, brilliant in its role as Downton Abbey, was hundreds of years old, but, based on what I found on the castle's website, Highclere Castle has stood in its current incarnation only since 1878 when the interior modeling was completed. I say *only since 1878* since, having visited Westminster Abbey in London, I now believe that everything in England is 1000 years old. That makes the current version of Highclere Castle a mere 36 years older than Pittock Mansion, which was completed in 1914. And the two houses may as well be kissing cousins since they have so much in common.

Unlike *Downton*'s Lord Grantham, Henry Pittock was, first, an actual person, and second, a self-made man. He was English born, Pittock, arriving in America at 19 "barefoot and penniless" (his words). Eventually, he took over the local newspaper, *The Oregonian*, then the *Weekly Oregonian*, and in time he built an empire. His house, Pittock Mansion, stands on 46 acres of land, and it is complete with glorious gardens, a greenhouse, and a servants' residence. I realized, as I admired the opulent furnishings, the family's living area, and the downstairs servants' hall, that wandering around Pittock Mansion was more than a tourist activity. It was research, a chance to stand in a grand house, to see the wide, winding staircase, to feel the sunlight (more like cloudlight in Portland) in the open, airy rooms. I was able to use my personal experience when I described the fictional Hembry Castle, and more than one room in Hembry Castle was inspired by rooms in Pittock Mansion.

I also visited England twice while writing *Hembry*. Most of the London locations in the story were chosen because they were places I've visited myself. I stood on the Victoria Embankment near the Houses of Parliament watching the River Thames roll. I've taken some of Edward's walks through the city. Many of the buildings are different (I'm pretty sure the Gherkin wasn't around in 1870), yet some are the same. Here in Las Vegas buildings are imploded if they are more than 20 years old.

In *On Writing Well*, in Chapter 13 "Writing About a Place," William Zinsser says that "next to writing about people, you should know how to write about a place" (94). He's talking about nonfiction writing, but a lot of what he says applies to fiction too. Every story, whether it's true or make-believe, happens somewhere, and it's the writer's job to make that somewhere believable.

Zinsser warns writers to avoid clichés when describing places. It's so easy to fall into the trap of using phrases we've heard before. Visiting the places I'm writing about helps me avoid those pesky clichés. That's not to say I never use them. I'm guilty of using the word "quaint," which Zinsser says is a no-no, but having walked up a grand marble staircase in a century-old house, I know how smooth the banister is and I know how hard it is not to trip on the oddly angled stairs.

During my visit to Pittock Mansion I noticed details specific to a grand house that can't be spotted in a brochure. I was able to make my descriptions personal—descriptions that only could have come from me—because I was there, I saw it, I walked it, I heard it. I can read about the weather all I want, but experiencing a rainy English day for myself makes it easier for me to describe it. Experience provides its own language. Experience opens us up and allows us to find the precise vocabulary to express what we see, hear, smell, taste, and touch. Specific street names, monuments, places of interest—those details can be found online. But standing there, absorbing the scenes, hearing the voices, tasting the local food, there's nothing like it.

My afternoon at Pittock Mansion and my two visits to England helped me shape *Hembry Castle* into the story I wanted to tell. Hembry Castle isn't simply my characters' residence. It's a living, breathing place. I know. I've been there.

IT'S KIND OF LIKE TIME TRAVEL: MY EXPERIENCE

And as imagination bodies forth
  The forms of things unknown, the poet's pen
  Turns them to shapes and gives to airy nothing
  A local habitation and a name.
  ~William Shakespeare, *A Midsummer Night's Dream*

When I first began writing historical fiction, I never thought to travel for research. I was content writing about places I had never been. I have an active imagination, as fiction writers do, and with photographs, maps, Google Earth, and other research, I was able to visualize the place I was writing about. Once I could picture the place in my mind I could describe it. I've written about southeastern Georgia, Nazareth, Jerusalem, and Salem, Massachusetts without setting foot in any of those places. It wasn't until I started writing *Her Loving Husband's Curse*, the second book in the *Loving Husband Trilogy*, that I made the decision to visit Salem.

I was prompted to take the trip because I felt as though I

had used up whatever I learned about Salem from my internet search while writing the first book. I needed new things to say for the second book, so on a whim I decided to visit Salem so I could see it for myself. Traveling to Salem was a lot like time travel to me, and that trip brought the next two *Loving Husband* books to life in a way I couldn't have without that first-hand experience. In Salem, you have elements of life from before the witch hunt hysteria in 1692, a sense of what life was like during the late seventeenth century, as well as the present-day vibe.

It was a surreal feeling when I first arrived because I had already spent so much time in Salem in my imagination. Hey, I might see James or Sarah walking the streets! Yes, I know James and Sarah are fictional characters, but they are my fictional characters, which makes them real to me (and hopefully to anyone who reads the books). The first thing I did when I arrived was take the red trolley around town. Salem is a walking town, but the red trolley is nice because the tour guides give extra insights—Salem FYIs, if you will. Did you know that Salem was originally called Naumkeag, after the native population that lived there? Or that Salem is likely a shortened form of Jerusalem?

There's a calm in Salem I can't associate with any other place. The coastline along the bay is scenic, the bay stretching out into the expanse of the Atlantic Ocean, the trees along the coast adding green to the blue of the water. Little boats bob in the waves, caught in the mud at low tide, and people wander along, some sightseeing, some enjoying the day. The beaches are popular, and families of moms, dads, children, and grandparents splash in the waves and sit in the sun.

After the trolley, my next stop was the Salem Witch Museum, near Salem Commons. First I saw the statue of Roger Conant, who arrived in 1626. The statue is raised several feet off the ground as Conant stares into the distance like a disapproving headmaster. Across the street is the Salem Witch Museum, a large brick building, a former church, in fact. The museum shows various scenes from the witch hunt tragedy. How does someone turn against a neighbor? A friend? A wife? All these years later we still don't know, and that's what makes the Salem Witch Trials both fascinating and frightening. We've seen similar circumstances happen again, and again, and again.

Imagine my surprise when, behind the Peabody-Essex Museum, I encountered the John Ward House built in 1684. Long brown wooden slats. Diamond-paned casement windows. Steep, pitched gabled roof. It looks exactly like the house I described as the one belonging to my character, James Wentworth. I knew this house though I had never seen it before except in my dreams. I took picture after picture to prove to myself that James' house, this house I created in my imagination, is real.

From James' house (excuse me, the John Ward House) I walked to Pickering Wharf, which also plays an important role in the story. From Pickering Wharf I walked down the block (everything in Salem seems to be down the block from everything else) to the House of the Seven Gables, made famous by the novel from Salem's favorite son, Nathaniel Hawthorne. From his cousin, Hawthorne learned the story of the old house, which served as the inspiration for his book. The house changed over time as it was remodeled and gables were added, along with the secret passage he made famous. Again, I felt myself pulled back in time as I examined the furniture and the wall hangings. Outside the house is the garden, a burst of pinks and purples. As I admired the flowers I saw the sea stretching out to the horizon. I even met a friendly black and white cat. I also visited Pioneer Village near the bay. In the village you pass meadow-like grounds of overgrown grass, weeds, trees, front yard gardens, and historically accurate replicas of the homes of the earliest English settlers. The costumed docents explain everything and answer questions. Pioneer Village was the closest to a complete immersion into the past I found in Salem.

Travel can create a space for discoveries that could have come only from our own observations. When we write we channel our knowledge and experiences through our individual perspectives. No one else can see a place though our eyes. Ten authors might visit the same location and each author will describe it differently. This is the glory of being a writer. We get to share our unique views with the world.

There is no checklist of things you must do when you travel for research. It might be helpful to know what you want to see when you arrive so you can plan your time accordingly. More often than not, though, it's the places you discover by accident, like Pittock Mansion in Portland, Oregon or Pioneer Village in Salem, Massachusetts, that provide the most value.

If we want our readers to experience time travel, then it helps if we have experienced time travel ourselves. It isn't always possible to travel for research, but if you can go, go. Whenever I can, I travel to the places I'm writing about. If nothing else, it's an excuse to see the world.

14

CREATIVE INSPIRATION: BOOKS, MUSIC, AND PINTEREST

If you must err, do so on the side of audacity.
  ~Sue Monk Kidd

Research doesn't have to be only about going through stacks of books and articles and taking endless notes. Make this time fun for yourself. Yes, traveling is a great way to make your research more interesting, but there are other things you can do to make the research process enjoyable.

Visit local historical sites or museums that are reminiscent of the period you're writing about. Read books and listen to music from that time. Watch movies or documentaries. I discovered the wonderful film *Gettysburg* while researching my American Civil War story. Watching the soldiers march and hearing the battle calls helped me recreate similar scenes. I also listened to music from the era. I must have listened to the soundtrack for Ken Burns' *Civil War* documentary a hundred times. I even bought a children's paper doll book with Civil War uniforms and, yes, I played with the paper dolls and folded the clothes over the soldiers. I had no trouble describing the uniforms—or the garments underneath— while I was writing. When I wrote *Victory Garden* I watched silent films and listened to ragtime music.

There's a joke I've seen, a cartoon of a writer watching TV. The writer says, "I'm researching!" to the cynical-looking people nearby. As fiction writers, we know that watching TV or movies, reading books, or listening to music becomes part of our writing process. As fiction writers, we need to fuel our imaginations. We need to fill our creative wells so we have a brain bubbling over with ideas when we have empty pages to fill. Immersing ourselves in the culture of the period we're writing about is another way to dip into the past.

Here are some of the places I found creative inspiration while writing my Victorian story. I hope that by reading over my list you'll be able to begin a similar list of your own.

Books
Nonfiction:
Up and Down Stairs: The History of the Country House Servant by Jeremy Musson

What Jane Austen Ate and Charles Dickens Knew by Daniel Pool

How To Be a Victorian: A Dawn-to-Dusk Guide to Victorian Life by Ruth Goodman

The Victorian City: Everyday Life in Dickens' London and *Inside the Victorian Home: A Portrait of Domestic Life in Victorian England* by Judith Flanders

The Writer's Guide to Everyday Life in Regency and Victorian England From 1811-1901 by Kristine Hughes

To Marry an English Lord by Gail MacColl and Carol McD. Wallace

Below Stairs: The Classic Kitchen Maid's Memoir That Inspired "Upstairs, Downstairs" and "Downton Abbey" by Margaret Powell

The Essential Handbook of Victorian Etiquette by Thomas E. Hill

Fiction:

True, it's important to research the history when you're writing historical fiction, but often other novels will bring the past to life in a more visceral way than nonfiction history books. It's a good idea to read other historical novels set during your era. You may even discover ideas for your own story. As Justin Kleon says in *Steal Like an Artist*, if there's a good idea out there, it's okay to steal it and make it your own. Don't plagiarize, of course, but take something good and put your own spin on it.

Sometimes I'll find inspiration in a novel that isn't necessarily set in my time period but there's something about the story that provides me with ideas.

Here are some of the novels I read while writing *When It Rained at Hembry Castle*:

The Buccaneers and *The Age of Innocence* by Edith Wharton

Snobs by Julian Fellowes

The Remains of the Day by Kazuo Ishiguro

I read A LOT of P.G. Wodehouse (but really, can you read too much Wodehouse?)

I read A LOT of Dickens (but really, can you read too much Dickens?)

Wolf Hall and *Bring Up the Bodies* by Hilary Mantel (set in the Tudor era—I know—but I love Mantel's historical fiction)

Music:

Since my Victorian story is set in the 1870s, people were dancing to waltzes and polkas. Strauss and Chopin were favorite composers, which works well for me since I love to listen to classical music.

I was also able to find a few mp3s of Victorian-era music. Here are a few examples of what I found:

Victorian Dining by Peter Breiner and Don Gillis
Victorian Edwardian by Alexander Faris
Victorian Love Songs by Craig Duncan

Pinterest:

If you're not familiar with Pinterest, it's a social media site where you can find pins about pretty much any area of interest ranging from recipes to fashion to books. You can create a free account on Pinterest, and once you have an account you can create boards for your specific interests. You can make your boards public so others can see or you can keep them private for just yourself or those you invite. Pinterest has proven to be a useful place to discover interesting historical tidbits I use in my novels. *When It Rained at Hembry Castle* was the first novel I wrote since I started with Pinterest, so it was the first time I was able to use pins from the site to inspire my writing.

When I needed to describe the sitting room at Hembry Castle, I went to my research board, found the pin for the photograph I wanted to use as inspiration, and then I described what I saw. I pinned photographs of furniture, curtains, and rugs. I pinned photographs of Victorian clothing and hairstyles. I pinned Victorian recipes. I created a private board for my research since I didn't want to bombard my Pinterest followers with my many research pins; then, when I had everything I needed, I created a public board so readers could see the inspiration behind the story.

I enjoyed the cultural research for the *Loving Husband Series* as well. There are many books about the Salem Witch Trials, but I had to dig a bit to uncover the specifics of people's day to day lives during that time.

Not only did I have to understand seventeenth-century Salem and the witch hunts, I also had to decide how I would write a supernatural character since James Wentworth is of the preternatural persuasion—a vampire, to be exact. All authors who write about anything fantastical—vampires, witches, werewolves, mermaids, time travel, whatever—get to define the boundaries of their magical worlds. If you're writing historical fiction, then you need to define that magical world within the boundaries of your historical story. That's why world building is so much fun. Anything goes as long as we, the authors, make our worlds believable. A story can be fantastical and believable at the same time. Read the *Game of Thrones* books, or watch the TV show, if you want proof.

Here are some of the cultural resources I used when writing *Her Dear & Loving Husband*. Again, I hope my list inspires a list of your own.

Children's Books:

I love to use children's books as sources. Children's books state the information clearly, concisely, and if you're inspired by drawings and photographs as I am, the illustrations in children's books are great visual aids. Look at it this way—you get to look at pretty pictures and call it research.

When I was writing *Her Dear & Loving Husband* I happened upon a children's book called *Samuel Eaton's Day* by Kate Waters about a day in the life of a boy in Colonial America. The pictures for *Samuel Eaton's Day* are photographs of actors portraying the events, which allowed me to visualize how the colonists lived.

I also read *The Witch of Blackbird Pond* by Elizabeth George Speare. I loved that book when I was younger, and I still do. While the novel isn't about the Salem Witch Trials, it is about witch accusations in Colonial America in the seventeenth century.

Nonfiction:

The Salem Witch Trials: A Day-by-Day Chronicle of a Community Under Siege by Marilynne K. Roach

Six Women of Salem by Marilynne K. Roach

Death in Salem: The Private Lives Behind The 1692 Witch Hunt by Diane Foulds

Vampire Forensics: Uncovering the Origins of an Enduring Legend by Mark Collins Jenkins

Fiction:

I read some vampire fiction for *Her Dear & Loving Husband* since I wasn't familiar with the vampire genre. I wanted to see what other authors had done with their paranormal characters.

The Twilight Saga by Stephenie Meyer

Dead Until Dark (Sookie Stackhouse Book 1) by Charlaine Harris

Interview With a Vampire by Anne Rice

Dracula by Bram Stoker (who can avoid this classic when reading about vampires?)

The Passage by Justin Cronin

Once Bitten by Kalayna Price

For more inspiration for the Salem Witch Trials, I read:

The Crucible by Arthur Miller

The Scarlet Letter and *The House of the Seven Gables* by Nathaniel Hawthorne

Daughters of the Witching Hill by Mary Sharratt

Music:

Music was a challenge with *Her Dear & Loving Husband*. Although I didn't include any music in the story itself, it was always in the background since I listened to a lot of music while writing.

Since I was writing about the Salem Witch Trials, I was writing about Puritans in the Massachusetts Bay Colony. In such a stern society that placed all its hope in the afterlife, music played little role other than church hymnals, if even those were sung. I've read conflicting accounts: some say they sang hymnals, others say they didn't since even church music represented too much of an earthly pleasure.

Quick Write:

Now it's your turn. Where might you find cultural inspiration for your historical story? Which books, fiction or nonfiction, might provide ideas and insights? What music can you find from your era? Are there local historical sites, museums, gardens, or other cultural places of interest you might visit? Can you find pins on Pinterest that help you describe various aspects of your story?

15

CREATIVE INSPIRATION: TV AND FILM

History tells us what people do; historical fiction helps us imagine how they felt.

~Guy Vanderhaeghe

TV and film can also serve as inspiration for our historical stories. Like the writer in that cartoon, we can watch TV shows, films, and documentaries and call it research.

Here are some of the TV shows and films I watched while writing *When It Rained at Hembry Castle*. As with fiction, some of what I watch is set in the era, some is not, but all of it stirs my imagination in one way or another.

Downton Abbey (surprised, right?)

Upstairs, Downstairs

The Buccaneers

North and South

Lark Rise to Candleford

Cranford

Pride and Prejudice (Colin Firth's version)

Sense and Sensibility (Emma Thompson's—and Alan Rickman's—version)

I tried to watch the TV versions of *Bleak House* and *Great Expectations*, but screen adaptations of Dickens' work rarely thrill me. They get the drama down all right, but you'd never guess Dickens was one of the funniest authors in the English language from the dreariness of the adaptations. I did a little better with *Dickensian*, if for nothing else but Stephen Rea's performance as Inspector Bucket. I do believe we've hit the jackpot with the latest film version of *David Copperfield*, which finally captures Dickens' comedy.

Keeping Up Appearances—Another Bucket (It's BooKAY).

Miss Fisher's Murder Mysteries—this Australian show is set in the 1920s, but I love Essie Davis' Phryne Fisher so much I'll use any excuse to watch it. Phryne Fisher's clothes are even more fabulous than the costumes on *Downton Abbey*.

Television and film also helped while I wrote *Her Dear & Loving Husband* and then again when I wrote the prequel, *Down Salem Way*. To get into the flow of life in the Massachusetts Bay Colony, the first thing I did was rewatch *The Crucible*, a story I've loved since high school. It was helpful seeing the period costumes, the wooden houses, the horse-drawn carriages, and the farming since I could then visualize what I was writing about.

If you shop online, you're familiar with those lists of "If you like this, you'll like this…" After I watched *The Crucible* another title popped onto my TV screen—*Three Sovereigns for Sarah*. I wasn't familiar with this movie starring Vanessa Redgrave, but the 1985 film is the perfect companion to *The Crucible* since *Three Sovereigns for Sarah* is also about the Salem Witch Trials. The main difference is that *Three Sovereigns* is based on factual accounts; in fact, much of the dialogue in the film comes directly from transcripts from the trials.

Three Sovereigns is about three sisters—Rebecca Nurse, Mary Easty, and Sarah Cloyse (played by Redgrave)—caught in the horror of the witch hunts. Rebecca and Mary are hanged after their witchcraft convictions, but Sarah survives since she was jailed away from the others due to overflowing prisons. Twenty years later, seeking to clear her sisters' names, Sarah is given three sovereigns, one for each sister. There are also a number of documentaries about the Salem Witch Trials, and each one provided interesting insight.

Everything I watch for research adds some new perspective that I wouldn't have otherwise considered. All of it is important when crafting a story.

Quick Write:

What television shows, documentaries, or films can you find about your chosen era? Make a list of everything that looks interesting and take some time to start watching them. Don't forget to add interesting tidbits to your notes.

CREATIVE INSPIRATION: PEOPLE

People have this nostalgic idea that the past was better, but the truth is most folks had very hard lives.
   ~Isabelle Allende

Occasionally, I stumble across a real-life person who, although this person may not become a character in my novel, helps to bring my story to life in a way I hadn't envisioned. This happened when I discovered Anne Bradstreet while writing *Her Dear & Loving Husband*.

   I discovered Bradstreet through a roundabout route, which happens often when I'm writing historical fiction. I had been thinking that since my characters James and Elizabeth live in Salem in 1692, and since James is the bookish type who leaves his studies at Cambridge to follow his father to the Massachusetts Bay Colony, he would likely spend his free time reading. What would he read by the firelight of his hearth in 1692? As I searched for popular literature during the late seventeenth century, I happened upon the name

Anne Bradstreet. I was surprised that I hadn't heard of her. I had taken American literature classes for my English degrees, but I hadn't been introduced to Bradstreet's work.

Bradstreet was born in England in 1612. In 1630, she emigrated with her wealthy family to the Massachusetts Bay Colony. The family lived in various places around Massachusetts, including Salem, and her father and her husband both helped to found Harvard College. Bradstreet was the mother of eight children, a wife, and a poet at a time when the first two were considered all a women need be in this world. She became the first English person in North America to be published, and it's rumored that King George III had a book of her poetry in his collection.

As I read Bradstreet's poems, I was impressed with the depth of feeling she shares in her work. Since she was a Puritan, I assumed that her work would be all about praising God, and she certainly shares that sentiment in much of her poetry. Then I found the poem that helped me shape the novel I was writing: "To My Dear and Loving Husband."

If ever two were one, then surely we.
If ever man were loved by wife, then thee.
If ever wife was happy in a man,
Compare with me, ye women, if you can.
I prize thy love more than whole mines of gold,
Or all the riches that the East doth hold.
My love is such that rivers cannot quench,
Nor ought but love from thee give recompense.
Thy love is such I can no way repay;
The heavens reward thee manifold, I pray.
Then while we live, in love let's so persever,
That when we live no more, we may live ever.

As soon as I read the poem I knew it could serve as the missing link I had been searching for to connect the different plots in my story. Bradstreet's poem even provided me with the novel's title, *Her Dear & Loving Husband.*

This is the kind of synchronicity—meaningful coincidence—that makes writing fiction the greatest thing on earth as far as I'm concerned. There's a moment when these disconnected pieces come together through some random discovery, and suddenly the story makes sense, the picture becomes clear, and I can finally see the novel I meant to write in the first place.

Quick Write:

There is more than one way real-life people can inspire your story. For example, Anne Bradstreet herself is not a character in my novel, but her poem plays an important role. What have you learned about real-life people that might help you bring your story to life? Keep track of everything. You never know what might prove to be useful.

MOVING PAST THE BLANK PAGE

There's no such thing as writer's block. If you're having trouble writing, well, pick up the pen and write. No matter what, keep that hand moving. Writing is really a physical activity.
~Natalie Goldberg

One of the hardest parts about writing historical fiction, or any fiction, or any writing for that matter, is simply getting started.

Inertia is powerful. So many people want to write. So many people say they have a story they feel compelled to tell but they never quite get around to it. I have a friend who has wanted to write mystery novels for as long as I've known her. She reads mysteries and she reads books about how to write mysteries. She belongs to Sisters in Crime, a cool group for women crime writers. Yet she hasn't written anything. When I ask her about her novel, her answer is always, "One day I'll actually do it."

Writing is one of those things that's so easy not to do.

Finding the momentum to start a new project can be over-whelmingly difficult. There are no tricks to finding motiva-tion, finding a way past the Excuses, or even sitting down to the computer. In *Bird by Bird*, Anne Lamott tells a story about Natalie Goldberg, who, when asked what the trick was to writing, mimed writing across a yellow pad. These days you might mime typing your fingers across a keyboard. No matter how you write, that essential truth remains: in order to write you must write. That's it. I wish I had some magic formula for writing motivation. If I did I'd bottle it, sell it, and buy the first bottle myself.

I hate writing first drafts. I well and truly hate it. I hate writing first drafts of anything—historical novels, essays, scholarly articles, blog posts, short stories, emails. This chap-ter. I have rewritten grocery lists because I didn't like the way I organized them. When I'm teaching writing I always know what to say to help my students deal with first draft phobias or writer's block, but do I listen to my own advice? Some-times—if I'm lucky. There's a reason why Ernest Hemingway and Anne Lamott refer to them as shitty first drafts. They are, in fact, shit. But as Lamott points out, they must be written or else there is no second, third, or final draft.

Talking myself out of writing a first draft is a particular talent of mine. I fall victim as much as anyone else to those old writers' standbys known as Excuses. It's not hard to find plenty of Excuses to keep from working. First draft days are days when I dust and vacuum instead of writing, you know, not regular maintenance house cleaning but vacuuming-behind-the-sofa-where-people-will-never-see kind of clean-ing. The days when I brush my cat instead of writing that first draft, or worse, talk to my cat instead of writing that first draft. She doesn't answer so it's fine. There are grocery stores to shop in, books to read, classes to teach. I even exercise instead of writing, and I hate exercising. The list of Excuses can be endless.

The first thing you need to examine if you're stuck is whether or not the writing project you're working on really gets your creative juices flowing. Ultimately, this is what finally gets me going. I realize that I'm so interested in my subject that I'm able to overcome the inertia and start writing.

Taking time to get your thoughts straight before you start writing can be helpful. Brainstorming and prewriting are two exercises that have helped me rev up my writing mojo when I felt my tank was empty. What's nice about brainstorming and prewriting is that they are open-ended activities and there's no right way to complete them. The purpose is to create ideas for your story. It's much easier to get started when you have some sense of what you're going to be writing that day.

A lot of writers like to skip the brainstorming/prewriting part, but I recommend taking the time to think things through. The more ideas you have, the easier it will be to push past the difficult first draft.

One of my favorite ways to brainstorm is called the Quick Sketch. I use this activity with my writing students. The Quick Sketch helps writers find some sense of the arc that will guide them through the beginning, middle, and end of their stories.

A Quick Sketch is easy to complete. Take a blank sheet of paper, or you can do this digitally on a computer if you prefer. Divide the paper into thirds and label the first part Beginning, the second part Middle, and the third part End.

Remember, there is no right way to do this. It amazes me how students of all ages get so stressed over making mistakes about how they fold the paper. People are obsessed with getting things just right. There is no "just right" here. Relax.

This is for your own use. This activity is simply a tangible way to work through your thought process. If you do this on three old dinner napkins it's all good. You can use lined paper or not use lined paper. You can do this on one sheet of paper or use an entire sheet for each section.

Leave space in each of the three sections for both writing and drawing. Yes, you read that correctly. Drawing. Remember that thing we used to do when we were young and uninhibited? Again, I won't bore you with the research, but there are studies that show how drawing helps our brains understand better. I studied storytelling and creativity for my Ph.D. dissertation, and both are fascinating subjects. Drawing is another thing people get all worked up about because they don't draw like artists. Take a breath. It's okay. No one is going to see this but you. You're not creating something that will be displayed in a museum. Draw stick people. I do.

Your task with the Quick Sketch is to sketch out through writing and drawing what you think is going to happen in the beginning, middle, and end of your story. Notice I said *what you think is going to happen* because any and all of these ideas are subject to change as you come to know your characters and your plot better. You can either write first or draw first. I usually write first and then draw, but if you'd rather draw first then write, that's cool.

You don't have to fill out the Quick Sketch in order. I usually know the ending of my story first, so I fill out the End section and then go back to the Beginning and the Middle as I figure out how I'm going to get to the ending. You can also add notes about what historical information you might need in each section. Actually, you can add anything you want to the chart, anything that helps you think through your story. This is your chart.

I've also had writing students fill out a KWL chart. The

KWL chart is a simple way of gauging your knowledge on any topic. Take a sheet of blank paper, or you can do this on the computer. Again, divide the paper into thirds or use three separate sheets of paper. Whatever floats your boat. Label one section K, the next W, and the third L.

In the K section, answer the question: What do I **know**? In the W section, answer the question: What do I **want** to learn? In the L section, answer the question: What did I **learn**?

I use the KWL chart to keep track of my historical information. What do I know about the era I'm writing about, what do I want to learn about it, and then after I've gone through the research process I fill in what I learned. The chart is an easy way for me to keep track of my progress. Most of my writing students use their KWL charts the same way, but some use it to help plan out their story since they prefer answering these questions to filling out the Quick Sketch.

If you're looking for some general historical fiction brainstorming prompts, try these:

1. Which era of history are you writing about? Be as specific as possible. A topic like the American Civil War is broad, but a subject like the battle at Gettysburg works well.

2. What is the setting of your story? Where specifically will it take place?

3. Who is your main character?

4. Who are your supporting characters?

5. Who is your antagonist?

6. What is the problem your main character(s) will be facing?

7. How will the problem be resolved? How will your story end? What is the last image the reader will take away from your story?

8. What is the theme or deeper meaning of your story?

9. How does your main character change from the beginning of your story to the end?

10. How many pages a day will you write?

11. How will you organize your schedule in order to find time to write?

12. How will you deal with writer's block?

This last question might seem odd, and it is, but if you have a plan in place when writer's block hits, and it will, it helps to alleviate the anxiety on those days when you can't remember how to spell your name.

Sometimes free writing helps me break through the first draft blues. Free writing is exactly what it sounds like—you're free to write whatever comes to mind. Some writers use a timer, set it for 10, 15, 20 minutes, and either type or handwrite whatever occurs to them during that time. You can write about your historical story or you can write about anything else. The point isn't what you're writing—the point is that you're writing. As Natalie Goldberg says, writing is a physical activity, and writing itself, writing anything, can get the juices flowing.

Free writing was a great help to me when I was writing *Victory Garden* and I was completely stumped for the beginning. I knew the ending, as I usually do, but I didn't know where to start. I tried this beginning and that beginning and nothing was working for me. I became so frustrated I didn't touch the manuscript for weeks. Finally, one day I started free writing about the women fighting for the vote. I wasn't writing a scene or anything in particular. I just imagined my main character in a room with other women fighting for the vote and I wrote what I saw.

As I was free writing I remembered a tidbit from my research, the day when women from the suffrage movement went to the White House to meet President Woodrow Wilson, so I incorporated that into my passage. After a bit of revising and editing, I ended up with what did in fact become the beginning of the novel. The women at the White House scene was even published separately as a short story in a literary journal. From nothing I got a whole lot of something, all from some random free writing where my only intention was to get myself going.

I'm also a big fan of Anne Lamott's idea for short assignments. In *Bird by Bird*, Lamott shares the idea of writing what you can see through a one-inch picture frame—one paragraph where you describe a scene from your story. Short assignments take away the inherent fear that comes with tackling a project.

When you think, "I want to write a historical novel about the fall of Rome," the grandness of the task can be paralyzing. If you say instead, "I'm going to write a paragraph describing Rome burning," that is doable. For my first drafts, I have a 500 word a day goal to meet. Five hundred words may not sound like a lot, but it's enough to move the story forward and not so much that it feels overwhelming. As soon as a first draft feels overwhelming I'll avoid it with every Excuse I have, and I have plenty of them, I promise you. If the juices are flowing I'll keep writing. Other times getting to that 500th word feels like root canal. Once I've met my 500 words, though, I can feel good because I met my goal. When I'm writing a first draft my main priority is to make progress every day, and 500 words works for me.

Oscar Collier suggests writing three pages a day, which, if you're typing on double-spaced pages, works out to about 750 words. Some people give themselves a 1000 word a day goal. Yes, you'll read articles about people who write 5000, 10000, even 15000 words a day. If that's you, cool. For the rest of us, short, attainable assignments can make the difference between whether or not our historical stories get written.

Other get-yourself-going activities include mind maps, bullet points, or the character sketch we'll look at in a later chapter. The point now is to gather ideas so you have something to work with when you sit down to write. Sometimes I keep a writing journal where I keep track of everything about my current work in progress that occurs to me. When I'm stumped I pull out my journal and review the ideas I've already come up with, and then I'll use some of those ideas as the basis for my writing that day.

A schedule can also help since you have already carved out a certain amount of time each day for writing. Some writers wake up early to get their writing done before they start the rest of their day. Others write at night when the house is quiet. I tend to work on my fiction during the late afternoon hours (around 3 pm-ish). Find the time that works for you, but you have to make a commitment to write during that time.

I'm a big believer that if you want to write badly enough then you'll make time for it. How many times have you been watching TV or scrolling through social media when you could have been writing instead? I'm as guilty of that as anyone. To help you meet your daily word count, you should limit distractions. I know some writers who use an app to restrict their internet access during their writing time. Some writers learn to ignore the temptation to check their emails. Turn away from social media, put your phone on airplane mode, walk away from the TV. Tell your cat you'll talk to her later. Hold your writing time as sacred because it is. And then you should be proud of yourself when you complete your word count for the day. There are so many other ways you could have spent your time, but you made the decision to work on your historical story. Hurrah!

It doesn't matter how you get yourself going. It only matters that you get going. Otherwise, that great historical story you want to share will never be told.

18

HOW TO WRITE A STORY

If history were taught in the form of stories, it would never be forgotten.
  ~Rudyard Kipling

This is how I begin writing a historical story, or any kind of story, really.

First, I notice when I have an idea that might become a story. The ability to recognize potential story ideas is a skill most writers learn at one point or another. We all have random thoughts that float through our minds at any given time of the day. For writers, these ideas are necessary for our sanity since these ideas give us something to write about. Play around with these ideas and decide which are passing through, perhaps on their way to someone else, and which have latched onto your heart and plan on sticking around.

Second, I daydream. Daydreaming is necessary for fiction writers—for most artists, really. Or at least that's what I tell people when I spend hours staring out the window, or at the wall, or at the cat, or anything else nearby. Sometimes, only occasionally, I may talk to myself. I don't answer so it's fine.

For me, the daydreaming period is as important as the hours I spend writing the book. I need this time to get a feel for who the characters are, how they respond in various situations, and what it feels like to live during their time. Without imagination, there is no land of make-believe, no living, breathing people to inhabit our worlds, and no sense of the time or place in which they live.

Next, if I'm still compelled by these characters after spending time in their worlds, I'll begin brainstorming ideas. I allow my imagination the run of the house during this time. This is where I use the Quick Sketch or a KWL chart. Sometimes I'll make a bullet point list. Sometimes I'll do a mind map of my various ideas, filling up my page or screen with any and all thoughts, no matter how random or silly they seem. Other times, I'll write my ideas into my journal.

However I brainstorm, I'll write what I think I know about the characters, what I think I know about the time period, and any story ideas. This is also where I'll do my preliminary research into the era. This first toe-dipping into the history allows me to picture my characters during this time and often, as I learn more about the people and events of the time, I come up with new ideas. At this point I'll write an outline.

We see these quizzes online—are you a plotter or a pantster?—and we're supposed to fit neatly into one box or the other. If you're not familiar with the terms, a plotter is a writer who plots out the story before writing and a pantser is someone who "flies by the seat of their pants" and goes with the flow, writing whatever part of the story they want without a plan. I would venture to guess that most writers fall somewhere in between. I certainly do. The logical part of my brain needs structure, at least to begin, so I'll write an outline of what I think will happen before I start my first draft. Again, I said what I *think* will happen because more often than not my outline changes as I continue writing. I'm not worried about a chapter by chapter breakdown at this point. I want a general feel for the story. More than the beginning, more than the middle, at this point I'm searching for the ending of the story, the conclusion that makes me sit up and say, "Yes! This is what my story is about!"

In other words, the first thing I want to know is my ending. Odd, perhaps, for some, but for me, if I know how the story ends then I can create a beginning and middle that brings me to where I want to be. Through trial and error and fried brain cells, eventually I'll hit on the last line of the novel. Once I have that last line I can construct a road map that will lead me, and the readers, through. A different way may work better for you. I know writers who prefer to be surprised by the ending as they discover it organically through the writing process. I know writers who focus first on the beginning because they feel it gives them a solid basis for the rest of the story. As with everything else to do with writing, you need to discover your own best way.

Once I have a general outline then I'll do my best to break down what I think I know about the story into a chapter by chapter outline. Even as I'm writing the chapter outline I know my ideas are fluid and the outline will change as my understanding deepens. Once I have my chapter outline, then I'll write my first draft.

After I finish my shitty first draft I'll put it away, preferably for a couple of weeks, sometimes longer if I have other projects I'm working on. By putting the novel away I'm able to put distance between myself and what I've written, which is necessary for an honest assessment of what I actually have on paper and not what I *think* I have on paper.

As writers we get so caught up in our own heads we forget that people who aren't us are going to be reading our stories and they need to understand what is happening. Our readers are not in our heads. It's scary enough for me in here. I wouldn't want to subject anyone else to the oddities of my headspace. Without some distance, I'm too close to what I've written to see it with the critical eyes I need to make judgments about what works and what doesn't. If you've been taught, as many writers have, to keep your creator and your editor separate, then now, when you're ready to embark on your second draft, is the time to pull out your editor's hat (which looks like a fedora to me). Now is the time when you have to be brutally honest about what you have written.

Is your story too long? Too short? Are the characters well developed? Does the story flow? Are there enough details? Too many details that weigh your story down? Are there unnecessary words in your dialogue? You want to examine the elements of your historical story by making sure your plot is strong and well-paced and your characters are believable. For historical fiction, you also want to make sure you have enough details that place your story firmly in its era without overwhelming the reader with an information dump.

How do we do this, exactly? We can study fiction writing skills from books or courses. We can study our favorite historical novels and see how the masters do it. That's really the best way to learn. Tear your favorite historical novels apart (I mean that figuratively rather than literally, but hey, whatever works) and see how your favorite authors do it. What is the first sentence? How do they introduce their characters? How do they make you feel as though you've traveled to the past? How do their stories end? By studying well-written historical fiction we can see how to construct our stories in an entertaining way that will keep readers engaged, which is always our primary goal as novelists.

I am absolutely brutal when writing my second draft. I know that most of what I wrote in my first draft will not make it to the final draft. That's okay. That time is not wasted. My mind needed to work through everything in order to figure out what my story is actually about. What took me three pages to say in a first draft can be condensed into a sentence or two so the rest gets deleted. Is that hard—deleting what might amount to hours of work? Yes, as a matter of fact it is, but it's necessary. Don't keep something simply because you wrote it. Professional writers understand that writing is a process, and those unnecessary phrases in your first draft were part of the process that allowed you to discover the best way to tell your story.

For me, my first drafts tend to be on the short side because the first draft is simply my way of working through the story. Really, my first drafts aren't much more than fleshed out outlines with some dialogue thrown in. I'm not even particularly concerned with the amount of historical detail I have in the first draft. I'll simply put (parentheses) in places where I know I'll need to fill in the blanks with more information specific to the era.

When I reread my first draft, I find that my writing is repetitive since I tried several times to say what I'm trying to say. As I write my second draft, I delete a lot because I'm getting rid of the excess. At the same time I'm filling in the historical details I skipped in my first draft. I tend to add a lot to the second draft; after all, you never know what might turn out to be important. As a result, my second draft is too long.

So my first draft is too short and my second draft is too long. In my third draft I whittle the manuscript down to its essential elements. As a result, my third drafts tend to be closer to just right. For example, my first draft of *Her Dear & Loving Husband* was about 60000 words, my second draft nearly 100000 words, and my third draft 86000 words, which was the final word count.

At some point, usually the third draft stage, I discover the story I meant to tell in the first place. Sometimes, it may take longer than three drafts. Then it becomes a matter of editing and making sure everything is right. What is right? That's up to you, the writer.

As for my style of prose, I make stylistic choices based on the fact that writing is my artistic expression. I've dabbled in painting and art journaling, and I love coloring books. Still, writing is my art. My literary idols are Charles Dickens, Toni Morrison, and Walt Whitman. On the surface they seem an odd bunch, but they aren't. They have a poetic fluidity in common, and this is what I try to emulate in my own writing. Do I get there? Not even close. I've ended up with a style that is part literary and part genre, and I'm proud of it because it's mine. That's how we becomes artists. We're influenced by what we love, and if we work hard and give it time our influences morph into something that is uniquely our own. This is what works for me. For you, well, you have different influences than I do. Study those influences and work with them until you find a style that is all yours.

It won't happen overnight. Think of Malcolm Gladwell's 10000 hour rule. I'm paraphrasing here, but Gladwell says it takes 10000 hours at something to become good at it. I've been writing for a long, long time so I passed the 10000 hour mark a long time ago. My point, and I do have one, is that my choices are based on what feels artistically correct. I understand that not all readers will like all of my choices, but I'm okay with that. No matter how you write, not every reader will like everything you do. Not every reader in the world is your intended audience. Find the people who love the way you write and stick with them.

For example, in *Woman of Stones*, God is written as G-d because religious Jews believe that God's name is too holy to be bandied about like it's nothing. God is referred to indirectly (as in HaShem, which translates to The Name) or it's written as an acronym, such as YHWH, which is sometimes pronounced Yahweh, though there are those who say that we no longer know how to say God's name since the pronunciation was lost after the destruction of the Second Temple. I have also seen God written as G-d. Looking over my choices, I chose to use G-d since I believe it's the easiest on an English speaker's eyes. Where there readers who didn't like seeing it written as G-d? You betcha. But the majority of readers didn't think twice about it. Many even defended it because they understood why I made that choice. Could I have written it as God? Sure. But I chose to make that change because it felt more authentic to me, and when I'm writing historical fiction I try to keep my story as authentic as I can while still keeping the language friendly to present-day readers.

When is a story finished? The answer is different for every writer. For me, I know a story is finished when I can read it without wanting to change anything. In other words, I can read my own book like a reader instead of a writer.

While I'm sort of on the subject, I want to speak briefly about writing to a formula. There is nothing inherently wrong with writing to a formula, especially if you're new to writing fiction; in fact, some genres such as romance and mystery have certain expectations about how stories should unfold. A romance should have a Happily Ever After ending. In mysteries, the whodunnit should be solved. Maybe one of the reasons I'm drawn to historical fiction is because it defies any one style of writing.

Other than clearly placing your story in your chosen historical era, anything goes when writing historical fiction, which is both a blessing and a curse. It's a blessing because you're free to tell your story in your own way and it's a curse because you're free to tell your story in your own way. True, if you're writing a historical romance then you're bound to a degree by the conventions of the romance genre, but even there you have wiggle room. One of the most popular historical romances of all time, the *Outlander* series by Diana Gabaldon, smashes every romance genre convention you can think of, which is one of the things I like about her books. I like books that defy expectations because those authors are more imaginative than those who adhere strictly to the rules.

Writing to a formula may be a great way to start when you're new to writing fiction, but at a certain point you need to decide what you have to offer your readers that is different. If you're simply rehashing the same story over again because you're adhering to a formula, what reason do readers have to continue reading your books? Who are you? is a great question to ask yourself regarding the characters you're creating. But who are you as a writer? What is special about your historical story? Why should readers read your book when they have so many others to choose from? As a writer, you should be able to answer these questions.

As writers have become more concerned with the business aspects of writing, they have become afraid of exploring, of playing, of imagination. They want the magic formula that will allow them to sell a million books so they can leave their dreaded day jobs. A number of years ago, when indie publishing first came into its own, stories abounded of authors selling boatloads of books and making boatloads of money. As a result, people thought that writing books was easy money. Go figure.

I'm not saying that it's not possible to make a living writing books. Of course it is. I am saying that writing books and writing books that people want to read are not the same thing. You need to discover what you have to offer that is uniquely your own. It's not a coincidence that many writers motivated by profit have dropped out of the publishing game because they didn't attract the readership they hoped for. Why? Well, there are a number of possibilities. Uninteresting characters, write-by-rote plots, bland narration, predictable stories that left readers with no reason to keep turning pages. You can follow a formula for writing fiction, but there is no formula that guarantees that readers will want to read what you write.

The loss of creativity is akin to the loss of personality, of uniqueness, of voice, of something special that could have only come from you. People want to stick to formulas, to worksheets, to a plan because on the surface it makes things easier. Maybe things are easier, but easier and interesting do not always go hand in hand. Creativity is a writer's greatest gift. Don't be afraid to use yours. Don't believe the argument that writing is either a business or a creative pursuit. It can be both. If you remember that then you're already ahead of the game.

And by the way, creativity has nothing to do with how fast you write. Some writers work quickly and tap into a wealth of imagination while others write boring stories at a snail's pace.

Some of the most successful novels, historical or otherwise, are the ones that took chances, left the formulas aside, and brought readers along on a spellbinding ride that was different, at least in some ways, from anything they had ever read before. What type of historical story will you write?

19

HISTORICAL FICTION IS FICTION

I hate writing but love having written.
~Dorothy Parker

The next two chapters cover the basics of creative writing. If you are already well-versed in fiction writing, you could certainly skip these two chapters. Some of us come to historical fiction with a strong writing background while others of us begin our historical fiction journeys without a lot of previous experience. If you're newer to writing fiction, here are some things to consider.

The basics of writing historical fiction are the same as writing any fiction. You need well-rounded characters that readers can connect to and you need a plot since your characters need something to do. There must be some kind of problem that your characters face. Again, if there is no problem there is no story.

Many writers are familiar with the long-standing debate over whether character or plot is more important. If you're into Greek philosophers, Aristotle believed that, when speaking of tragedy, plot is more important and character is secondary. Others, who are not Aristotle, argue that character is the most important. What is the answer? It's a trick question, of course. There is no right answer.

For me, I place more importance on character since my stories live or die on the strength of my characters. Not one reader has ever said to me, "I loved when that happened in the third chapter." Readers say, "I love James and Sarah" or "I was surprised by Richard." Perhaps you agree with Aristotle that plot is more important since to you it doesn't matter how interesting the people are if their problems are boring. I would venture a guess that the best stories have a good combination of both fascinating characters and intriguing plots.

If you're looking to break fiction down into its most basic parts, here are the four elements of storytelling:

1. The plot. This is the *what* of your story. The plot gives us actions and their equal and opposite reactions. The plot gives us causes and effects. The plot is the string of events that brings your character(s) from the beginning through the middle to the end of your story.

2. The characters. Your characters are the *who* of your story. The characters are the people who populate your historical world. They take the actions and make the decisions that drive your story forward.

3. The world. The world is the *where* of your story. Where does your story happen? What is the environment? During what era does your story take place? Is it winter, spring, summer, or autumn? What is the socio-economic reality during the time you're writing about?

4. The language. This is the *how* of your story. How will you share your story with your reader? What style of language, sentence structure, and word choice will you use? How will your characters speak?

When writing a story you should ask yourself the three questions that are taught in most creative writing classes: 1.) Who is my main character? 2.) What does my character want more than anything? and 3.) How can I prevent my character from getting it?

You never want to make things too easy for your character(s). I made that mistake with the first draft for a story I was writing called *The Vampire's Wife*. An eagle-eyed beta reader noticed that while it was a sweet story, it was boring because nothing much happened. The two romantic leads didn't have any problems. They met and fell in love and all was well. After all, they are my imaginary friends and I didn't want to make their lives difficult. But I understood what the beta reader meant and I knew she was right, so I found problems, a lot of problems, in the next draft of the novel that became *Her Dear & Loving Husband*. In order to have a page-turning story our characters must have obstacles to overcome.

Story Structure

Most writers are familiar with the three-act story structure. Your historical story should have a beginning, middle, and end. The first act is the set-up where you have some inciting incident that sets the tone for the rest of the story. The first major plot point of your story happens here. The second act is the rising action where things begin to get more tense for your character(s). More is on the line now, and the second major plot point of your story happens here. The third act is the resolution. The most important plot point of your story happens here.

There are various ways to understand story structure, and it helps to look at different versions because one might make more sense to you than others. Here is another version of story structure that I've shared with my writing students: Exposition, Rising Action, Climax, Falling Action, and Resolution. You can fit these five elements into the three act story structure or look at them separately. Either way works.

1. Exposition: The characters, setting, conflict, and any other important information are set up here. You don't want to go too heavy on the exposition in the beginning, however, since that will slow your story down. Give readers enough to understand what is happening. Just as you can overload readers with an information dump, you can overload readers with background information. A good tip is to start your story *in media res,* in the middle of things, and then fill in background information only where needed.

2. Rising Action: Problems begin to arise for your main character(s). You should include some surprises along the way because we don't want our stories to be too predictable. The best stories, even those that are not specifically mysteries, should have some element of suspense woven throughout. We want to keep readers turning pages. As Newton's Third Law of Motion tells us, for every action there is an equal and opposite reaction. Everything we do has repercussions. It should be the same for our characters.

Everyone struggles in one way or another. Sometimes our struggles are within us (internal conflict) and sometimes our struggles are caused by people and events beyond our control (external conflict). What types of conflict will your character(s) face?

Let's dig a little more deeply into conflict. There is person versus self, which is an inner conflict such as self-doubt or self-destructiveness. Remember that our protagonists (our main characters) don't necessarily have to fight an adversary (an antagonist). Our protagonists may well struggle against themselves.

Second, there is person versus person where the problem is with someone else. This is where an antagonist may come into the story.

Third, there is person versus society where there are problems between your characters and the societies in which they live. This is a common conflict in historical fiction.

Fourth, there is person versus nature where there are problems with the natural environment.

Fifth, there is person versus the supernatural where there are problems with paranormal or fantastical beings or events.

Finally, there is person versus technology, which is a conflict between your character(s) and science or technology.

Many novels have a combination of some of the above as a way to add tension. My stories tend to focus on person versus self conflicts while there are larger person versus society problems underlying the main story. But that's just me. You'll have a different focus for your stories.

3. Climax: What is the moment of greatest tension in your story? The climax is a turning point from which there is no going back. It's the most dramatic event of your story. Here, your main character faces her problem head on and the problem is solved in some way. This is what your story has been building up to.

4. Falling Action: This is the release of the story tension. If your characters have changed as a result of their experiences, this is where we see that growth. Remember, though, that not all characters change during the story. Just as we sometimes stubbornly stay the same no matter how the world changes around us, so too our characters might resist change.

5. Resolution: Finally, the ending. Not all stories have happy endings. Some will and some won't. Think about how to end your story in a way that is both true to the time period and your characters and satisfying for you and your readers.

Scene Sequels

Are you familiar with scene sequels? Neither was I until another writer introduced me to them. Scene sequels are a way to slow down and allow your characters, and your readers, time to think through what is happening. Scene sequels take place in four steps.

Step 1: Emotion

When an event happens your character has to react. After something happens we *feel* it first. Before rationality, before logic, there is emotion.

Step 2: Thought

After the emotion fades we think about what happened. Sometimes logically. Sometimes not. The intention is to make sense of the event. The thought stage is where the character questions what has happened, what should have happened, and what might happen in the future. If I do A, will B, C, or Z result?

Step 3: Decision

After the thinking is done, what will you do? Will Sarah run screaming from James when she discovers his secret? Will James tell Sarah what his secret is? This is the moment when the character forms a judgment based on his or her thoughts, making a decision one way or another.

Step 4: Action

This is the result of the decision. Once the decision is made, then the character has to do something about it. Sometimes the decision is to take immediate action. Sometimes the decision is to deal with it later. Sometimes the decision is to do nothing. But there should be some kind of culmination to the thinking and the decision.

The writer who introduced me to scene sequels told me

she keeps the formula on a sticky note on her computer to remind her of the steps while she's writing. The sequel is simple, four steps, yet it allows us to understand our characters on a deeper level. I think the reason the formula works so well is because it mimics our real-life process of dealing with problems. First we react in an emotional way, then we think about it, then we decide what to do, and then we do it (or we decide to do nothing, which is also a decision).

Scene sequels aren't something you want to use for every little event. But whenever something important happens, it's helpful to slow down and allow your characters time to feel, think, decide, and do. This will create a richer, fuller story for both your characters and your readers.

So how will you tell your story? Will you focus on characters or plot or both? Will you use scene sequels to allow your characters and your readers time to process events as they unfold? Deciding how you are going to structure your narrative is a big part of piecing together your historical story.

POINT OF VIEW AND VOICE IN
HISTORICAL FICTION

Writing is the painting of the voice.
  ~Voltaire

Here is a quick review of the different narrative points of view. The easiest way to understand narrative point of view is to think of it as a camera. The narrative point of view tells us where the camera is focused at any given moment in a story.

First-person narration is written from an "I" point of view. In first person, the narration is told through one character's viewpoint, as if we're seeing the story through that character's eyes, or as if the camera is showing us only what that character can see.

Second-person narration uses a "you" point of view. Nonfiction writers tend to use second-person narration more than fiction writers, but second-person narration can be used in fiction as well. Second-person narration is used to great effect by Spanish-language novelists.

Limited third-person point of view is a thinly disguised

first-person narrative. Limited third person uses "he," "she," "it," or "they" pronouns, but we're still only getting the point of view of one character at a time. Maybe the point of view character changes at different points in the story, but in each moment we only see the world through that one character's eyes.

Omniscient third-person narration is sometimes called "head-hopping" because the narrator can tell us the thoughts and feelings of every character in that scene, whereas in limited third person or first person we are limited to the thoughts and feelings of one character at a time. You can think of omniscient third person as a God-like narrator who can see into everyone's mind at once.

The point of view of the narration can help to determine the voice of your story. Of all the elements that go into writing historical fiction, voice is one of the most important. In order to fully immerse your readers into your era you should pay particular attention to the voice you're using.

Voice is personality shining through. Just as you have a unique speaking voice, so you have a unique writing voice. Of course, it's not quite so simple because you have to consider what voice works best for the story you're telling. The fiction voice I use changes because each story is different. In order to discover the right voice, I start by deciding who is telling the story.

Is the story written in first-person point of view? If so, who is the character telling the story? Is it written in third-person limited point of view? If so, then how will I show the thoughts and feelings of the point of view character through a distant narrator? Next, I consider the time period. A story told by a man living in Salem in 1692 is going to sound different from a story told by a woman living in Biblical Jerusalem.

When I'm teaching fiction workshops, voice is my favorite part to teach since voice is one of the facets of writing that could only come from the individual writer. There are many examples of historical fiction about the Tudor era, and many examples of novels about Anne Boleyn. The subject matter doesn't make the books different or special—it's the different voices created by the different authors.

Remember that voice in fiction isn't necessarily your voice, the author's voice, although it could be. If you're writing a first-person narrative, then it should be the character's voice bouncing off the page. If you're writing a limited third-person narrative, or even an omniscient narrative, there still needs to be some *there* there, a personality, a sense of a storyteller. The main trick to creating an authentic voice in fiction is understanding your narrator. In order to understand the narrator, you have to decide which point of view you'll use. See how they are connected?

Writing fiction is similar to being an actor. You need to place yourself firmly within the narrator's psyche. If you're writing from the point of view of Cleopatra, you need to imagine how she spoke, her mannerisms, her quirks, her biases. Why is she telling her story? How is she telling her story? Why would she choose to share these details of her life but not others? Research helps us understand the historical record, but you'll need your imagination to add flourishes so readers feel that Cleopatra is speaking to them.

Consider the tone you're trying to convey since tone contributes to voice. If you're writing a humorous story, the voice will feel different from the voice of a mystery (unless you're writing a humorous mystery). When I write third-person narratives, I write from a limited point of view. You might decide on an omniscient narrator who "head hops" and shares every character's thoughts. Which point of view should you choose? You should choose the point of view that feels right for your story. Not much of an answer, I know, but it's up to you to decide. Some writers love first person, some love third person, and some love the variety of deciding which point of view fits which novel.

One of the greatest lessons I've learned is that nothing is set in stone and I can change anything about my story at any time. Nothing is finished until I say it is, and that realization has been rather freeing. Once I discover the point of view and voice that work best for my story, suddenly the pieces of my story puzzle fit together and I can visualize the complete picture. That's when I'm in the flow of writing and there's nowhere else in the world I'd rather be. When I'm writing a first draft I flap about like a fish out of water (or an asthmatic without an inhaler—speaking from experience), spending hours writing long passages that have nothing to do with the story I want to tell. Every time I'm about to give up, though, I force myself to keep going because I've been at this long enough to know that the story will reveal itself eventually. How much hair I have by that time always remains to be seen, but bald or not bald, I know I'll figure out whatever it is that's not working. I have to relearn this whenever I start a new project, but mainly I have to relearn it whenever I start a story set in a new world. I have to constantly remind myself that I can experiment and play until I find the winning combination. After the heavy lifting is done, I can say I love having written.

Writing historical fiction has many similarities with writing any genre of fiction. All expectations for a well-crafted story still apply.

WHO ARE YOU? KNOW YOUR CHARACTERS

Writing historical fiction is a legitimate use of Multiple Personality Disorder.
~Peggy Ullman Bell

I was once asked in an interview how I developed such well-rounded, realistic characters. I didn't have a simple answer since I'm not entirely sure how it happens myself. Here I am, minding my own business as I think my way through a story, and suddenly these people appear. Who are you? I find myself asking the question aloud sometimes, to the amusement, or concern, of those around me. Sometimes these people appear fully formed and I know who they are from the moment I notice them. Sometimes it takes some work on my part to understand what they want with me. Mainly, I use my imagination.

Character inspiration can come from anywhere. Like story inspirations, your characters can be inspired by books, movies, TV shows, music, people you know, favorite actors, yourself, or your creativity.

I use the word character when I talk about fiction writing since that's the accepted way of referring to our imaginary friends. For me, it's more accurate to describe them as my people. My characters are my people. There's a disconnectedness to the word character, at least in my own mind, that doesn't fully describe what I'm doing when I write about my people. I want to write multi-dimensional beings who happen to be figments of my imagination. They are my imaginary friends, and I want them to become my readers' imaginary friends too.

My characters might emerge from a thought as vague as "I want to write about a woman fighting for the right to vote." And then, at some point, poof! There she is! Then I'll brainstorm ideas about this woman. Some ideas are keepers, some are not, but it doesn't matter at this point. I just need something tangible to mold. Ideas beget idea beget ideas. I find that my people reveal themselves when they are ready. If that sound a little woo-woo, well, that's because it is. There's an element of surprise in creating characters, which is why it's so much fun.

After several brainstorming sessions, I knew that my character, the woman fighting for the right to vote, lived with her father in New York City during World War I at the height of the fight for American women's suffrage. I already knew the book's title—*Victory Garden*, referring to the victory gardens planted during World War I and again during World War II —so I named her Rose Scofield (Scofield from the late, great actor Paul, who I imagined playing her father). I wanted that connection between Rose and the novel's title.

Rose is a school teacher and stubborn about wanting to live her life on her own terms. In fact, Rose Scofield is more than a bit like me. Did I intentionally work myself into Rose's character? Not at all. Maybe there was some aspect of myself I needed to examine through Rose. Maybe I subconsciously pulled ideas from the person I know best—me. One novelist friend said to me, and I tend to agree, that there's a piece of us in every character we create.

As with every other aspect of writing, there's no right way to discover who your people are. Some writers like to fill out character questionnaires. Some do free association brainstorming. Some think it through in their heads without writing anything down. Some like to begin by naming their characters.

I can't start writing about a character until I know that character's name. I always feel like the name is inherent in the character; in other words, the characters already know their names but they leave it to me to guess. I feel like the miller's daughter scrambling to guess Rumplestiltskin's name. Is it Bob? Is it Herbert? Is it Randolph or George or Ichabod? At some point, I do guess correctly, and that's without the help of a messenger spying on the One-To-Be-Named. I may have an idea or two before I know my characters' names, but it isn't until I know their names that I can really dig into what makes them tick.

Like actors, we have to understand the evolution of our characters. We have to know who our characters are, what they want, and how they grow (or don't) through the story. I always feel lucky when my people appear before me fully formed. That was the case with Olivia Phillips in the *Loving Husband Trilogy*. In her witchy way, she materialized out of the air.

When I began writing *Her Dear & Loving Husband* I knew nothing about present-day Salem, Massachusetts. Since I knew the story would go back and forth between the seventeenth and twenty-first centuries, I had to learn about Salem in its present-day reality. To my surprise, I discovered that twenty-first century Salem is a hotbed of modern mysticism.

Most places have some variety of shops that sell incense, books of spells, candles, and other mystical accessories. Such shops exist in abundance in Salem. I decided that my character Sarah Alexander would visit one. Who ran the shop? It should be someone Sarah knew, or was at least acquainted with. Being new to Salem, and not being one with an inherent belief in the mystical world, Sarah needed a push in that direction. That push came in the form of Olivia Phillips, who owns the psychic shop Sarah visits. I understood Olivia immediately. I saw her long gypsy skirts and large hoop earrings. I felt her motherly instincts and I knew the larger role she would play in the story.

When it comes to describing characters, I tend to cast favorite actors in the "part" of my people to help me get a sense of the characters' mannerisms and their cadences when they speak. As funny as this sounds, it works. Think about your characters and decide which actors you would cast in the roles, as if a movie producer asked for your dream cast. Imagine these actors in your scenes and write down everything you see and hear. You'll be amazed at how quickly your characters come to life. Charles Dickens used to run to the mirror to examine his own face as he made different expressions, and then he ran back to his desk to write down what he saw as a way of describing his characters.

By the way, the scene of Sarah's psychic reading at Olivia's shop was inspired by a real-life incident. My mother returned to university as an adult, and to fulfill a requirement she took a religious studies class. One of her assignments was to go to a psychic reading, and I went with her to see what it was like. The psychic was a young woman, about university age herself, and a lot of what she said was general and could have applied to anything. But then she said something about a move far away, which did startle me because I was planning on moving across the country and I don't recall having given away any clues in that direction. That psychic reading, with some modifications, ended up in *Her Dear & Loving Husband.* Here's another example of how you never know what real-life experiences will appear in your fiction.

The inspiration for my main character in *Woman of Stones* began when I read Anita Diamant's *The Red Tent.* I was blown away by Diamant's book. I love Diamant's poetic prose, her stream-of-consciousness storytelling, and her creative imagining of a Bible story from a woman's point of view. A Bible story from a woman's point of view? Cool. I love the way Diamant brought Dinah's story to life and I wanted to do something similar in a story of my own.

Part of my inspiration for the character of the Woman of Stones came from the way I chose to tell the story. *Woman of Stones* is a study in memory. I'm fascinated by memory, how we remember, what we remember, who we remember, what we forget, whether intentionally or not. I tapped into the stream-of-consciousness narration in Diamant's novel, and I love that poetic fluidity in Toni Morrison's novels as well. The novella became a first-person narration from the Woman of Stones. We follow her from her humble beginnings in Nazareth, to how she came to live in Jerusalem, to how she struggled on various levels. She tells her story as she remembers it. Sometimes she remembers in linear order and sometimes she doesn't. Her memories are fluid, jumping from here to there and back again as she struggles to make sense of her life. Through examining her life as a series of memories I was able to understand who she was and then share her story with others.

Sometimes when we're writing historical fiction we get so caught up in the history that we forget that in some ways people haven't really changed over time. How we dress has changed. Technology has changed. Medical knowledge has changed (thank goodness). But at our essence, people haven't really changed. What we want hasn't changed. We want our basic needs met. We want connectedness. We want to love and be loved. As Oprah Winfrey once said, we want to know that we matter. Sometimes we're selfish, and sometimes we're kind. Sometimes we're helpful, and sometimes we step over someone who needs us. Sometimes we're understanding, and sometimes we're not. What is true about people in Ancient Egypt is largely still true about people today. I find this aspect of human nature fascinating, and it's something I enjoy exploring through historical fiction.

This brings me to one of the more problematic parts of writing historical fiction: the historical beliefs and customs of the time we're writing about. While what people want is essentially the same, our social mores have evolved. Accepted beliefs during the late seventeenth century—or any century other than our own—may seem wrong to modern-day eyes. For example, for most of history, women were expected to be seen and not heard. I'd much rather be a woman today than any other time in history.

In Salem in 1692, under Puritan law, women couldn't speak for themselves. When a woman claimed to be attacked by someone's shape, a man had to file the complaint on her behalf. Women had no legal rights, and every aspect of women's lives was determined by men. There are times in *Down Salem Way* when James puts his foot down as the head of his small family. Though his wife bristles, she gives in, which would have been expected of a seventeenth-century goodwife.

Outlander author Diana Gabaldon said (and I'm paraphrasing here) that historical novelists are afraid to write about the truth of the past because that truth often doesn't fit with our current way of thinking. But if we're going to write historical fiction then we must be honest about people during the time we're writing about. In the seventeenth century, James is the head of his family and he has the right to prohibit Lizzie from attending the witch trials, which he does. The rum John Wentworth sells overseas is traded for human beings who are later sold as slaves. During the witch trials, family members accused each other of witchcraft, even when those claims resulted in the accused person languishing in prison or being hanged. It isn't pretty, but that's the way it was. If people want to read about perfect worlds where everyone is treated fairly and equally, then historical fiction is not for them. Probably most anything they read or watch is not for them.

As a society, we're still struggling with the same issues that have plagued us all along, with false accusations and gender and racial inequality being high on that list. If you're writing historical fiction and your characters act like they are in the twenty-first century in their manner of believing, speaking, and acting, then your historical story is in trouble. It can be painful to allow characters to act in a way that is truthful to the time, but you need to allow it to happen if you want your story to have authenticity. Yes, you can have characters who defy conventions. History is not often made by well-behaved people, after all, and there have always been those willing to buck the system to be true to themselves or to try to help others. But keep in mind that people who believed or acted differently than the norm often suffered persecution. Throughout history people have suffered serious consequences for being different in any way.

In historical fiction there are often characters who question the way things are in their time, characters who don't accept the status quo. In *Victory Garden*, Rose doesn't accept the fact that women can't vote so she fights for that right. Still, you should balance such characters with those who represent the accepted mores of that era. We are writing about history, not sugar-coated fantasies. People are complex. How about George Washington, one of the most revered figures in American history? Washington was a slave owner. Not only was he a slave owner, he was merciless in his attempts to recover his runaway slaves. George Washington did good things, amazing things, even, like founding a new country and leading its first government, and he did rotten things like keeping slaves. People are multi-dimensional, and our characters, our make-believe people, should be multi-dimensional too.

There are no secrets to creating characters. If an idea works it works and if it doesn't it doesn't. Eventually all the right characteristics will fall into place. Developing characters comes down to allowing our imaginations freedom, dreaming through our characters' traits, wants, and problems, allowing the characters to materialize in front of us, and then writing down what we see.

If you would like to answer questions as a way of understanding your characters, here are some for you.

Character Questionnaire

Answer the following questions as if you are your character(s). You can do this for your main character(s), antagonist(s), and supporting characters. Remember, what you write is not set in stone. You can change your mind at any time. If you fill out this questionnaire and later make new discoveries, allow yourself the flexibility to make those changes. This list was inspired by *Lessons That Change Writers* by Nancie Atwell, one of the greatest writing teachers as far as I'm concerned.

1. What is your name?

2. What era do you live in?

3. When were you born? Where do you live?

4. What is your biggest hope?

5. What is something odd about you? How are you different from those around you?

6. How old are you?

7. Who are your family?

8. Who are your friends?

9. What color hair and eyes do you have? How tall are you? Do you have any unique physical characteristics?

10. Who or what do you love?

11. What keeps you up at night?

12. What is your biggest challenge? Your biggest fear?

13. Why do you make the choices you do?

14. What is a secret that only you know?

15. What challenges do you face based on the time when you live?

16. What do you like about the era in which you live? What would you change about the era in which you live?

DID THAT WORD EXIST THEN?
LANGUAGE IN HISTORICAL FICTION

I love historical fiction because there's a literal truth, and there's an emotional truth, and what the fiction writer tries to create is that emotional truth.
    ~Jewell Parker Rhodes

By far, language is one of the biggest challenges when writing historical fiction. The style of language you prefer to write will likely reflect the style of language you prefer to read. As the executive editor of a literary journal of historical fiction, I have my own preferences.

At *Copperfield*, we don't want the pieces we publish to sound too modern. Some wonderful historical novelists do write with a more modern feel to their prose, and if you like that style then go for it. My personal taste, and the taste of the other editors at *Copperfield*, is for historical fiction to feel, you know, historical. Yet at the same time we need these historical stories to be accessible to modern readers, which means that using language that is wholly authentic to the period doesn't quite work, either. There is a middle ground in there somewhere, and it's our job as historical storytellers to find it.

When we receive submissions at *Copperfield*, the narrative style of the piece catches our attention in either a positive or a negative way. How do you find that balance between too modern and too authentic? By studying examples of historical language handled well and not so well by other novelists. You'll also need patience and practice.

In *Down Salem Way*, it was important to me that James' journal have the feel of being written in the seventeenth century, but only the feel of it. Language, both spoken and written, is musical whether we mean it to be or not. There's a rhythm, a cadence to language. As writers we need to catch the beat, so to speak, of the era we're writing about. If we can hear the melody then we're on our way to finding an authentic voice that won't put modern readers off.

While writing *Down Salem Way* I learned that the English language wasn't standardized in the seventeenth century. Some English language historians believe standardization began in earnest in the eighteenth and nineteenth centuries, crediting Noah Webster's spelling book in 1783 and his dictionary in 1828 with giving the English language some stability. Before that, punctuation was hit and miss. Spelling was whatever it was (which, perhaps, is not so different from today, to the lament of English teachers everywhere). To add to the confusion, some letters of the alphabet were used differently. For example, in the seventeenth century the letter I was used where today we would use the letter J, in line with the Latin use of I. During the years when *Down Salem Way* takes place, James could have been written as Iames. I get a headache just looking at that.

Here's an example of a love letter written in the seventeenth century that I found on Folgerpedia.com:

My best beloued cosen I am very glad to here from you, that you ar well, and I would haue you thinke that it tis one of the greates[t] comfordes I haue in this world to here of your well farer; I am very sory to here that your father is still in that humer of offering you more wifes; but as for this; shee hathe a greate porshone; wich I thinke if I hade; hee would not so much missl[i]ke of mee as hee dothe; and besides shee is honorabell wich dothe goe fare with most men nowe dayes; but I protest I writ not this out of any mistrust I haue of your loue; for I haue euer found it more then I haue desserued; yett I know not what shall deserue; and thus with my best wishes; for your good fortune; and happynes in all your bussines I rest euer –

your truly louing
frende while I breath
Jane Skipwith

Jane's letter is easier to read than it appears at first glance; even so, I wouldn't want to read an entire novel written like that so I wouldn't subject my readers to it. Some readers might not mind it, however, and if you want to try writing your historical novel in authentic language then give it a go. The final decision is yours. My call was to keep modern spellings except for a few words which had particular importance in the story, such as magick. I made that decision because I didn't want to write a novel that looked like it was written in a code that had to be deciphered. My task, as I saw it, was to allow James' words the rhythms of the seventeenth century without giving readers a conniption.

How did I accomplish that? Admittedly, it took some trial and error. I read a number of primary sources from the Salem Witch Trials. Transcripts from the trials themselves are available online, and there are other primary documents such as books and pamphlets from the era. I watched a few movies. I also paid particular attention to the words I used. Did this word exist then? Was this something James would have written in the seventeenth century? Nothing pulls readers out of a story faster than a misplaced word or phrase. James couldn't say, "Whazzup, dude?" in his journal. I mean, he could, but I would be banned from writing historical fiction forever after.

I decided to continue with words I had already used in *Her Dear & Loving Husband*. Examples would be the use of *aye*, *tis*, *twas*, and *afeared*, as well as *this day* for today. Also, during the seventeenth century the new year began on March 25, which is why *Down Salem Way* begins in 1691. Most historians, when they write about this era, begin the new year on January 1; however, since these are James' words, he doesn't recognize 1692 until March. Since I'm American, I used American spellings. As writers of historical fiction, we have to decide which aspects from the era we're going to use. We also have to decide *why* we're using them. We should always have a rationale behind our choices. Otherwise, our choices lack focus, and a lack of focus will seep into our stories and water them down.

To further immerse my readers in the seventeenth century, I used words that were common then, sprinkling them throughout the text for flavor. To accomplish that, I used Etymology Online, a tool recommended to me by a fellow historical novelist, Laurel Deedrick-Mayne. Etymology Online (www.etymonline.com) is a must-have resource for writers of historical fiction. With Etymology Online, you can type any word into the search box and it tells you what year the word came into use and where the word originated. I became obsessed with the etymology of words, and while I won't say I typed every single word of the manuscript into the website, I did type in a few. Actually, I checked a lot of them.

Not all of them. But most of them. One fun word I found was *dotard*, a word from the fourteenth century, which means, as you might expect, "imbecile, one who is in dotage or second childhood" (etymonline.com). Hilary Mantel uses the word in her Thomas Cromwell Trilogy, so I'm in good company. Using words specific to the period adds authenticity to your historical story.

You want to be aware of anachronisms, a frequent problem we see at *Copperfield*. Simply put, an anachronism is when something is misplaced in its historical context. My silly example of James saying, "Whazzup, dude?" would not work because, first of all, it's his diary so who would he be asking that question of anyway, and second, it isn't how someone would inquire after your well-being in the seventeenth century. As I used Etymology Online, I was amazed at how new some of the words I looked up were—new at least as far as the English language is concerned. Many words we use today were coined during the Jazz Age and others became popular in the 1940s during the World War II era. If you're writing something earlier than that be sure to double check your word choices to see if that word existed in the time you're writing about.

How do you find that balance between being historically authentic and still accessible to modern readers? How do you find that rhythm? Primary sources and watching television and films set during your era can help. If you're using TV or films as resources, be aware of over-exaggeration from some actors. Again, no names. Go back through your favorite historical novels and look specifically at the language. How does the author construct the sentences? What words specific to the era are used? Add examples to your notebook.

One novel I found helpful when I was writing *Down Salem Way* was *Daughters of the Witching Hill* by Mary Sharratt.

Daughters of the Witching Hill isn't set during the Salem Witch Trials, but rather in 1612, in England, when seven women and two men from Pendle Forest were hanged as witches. From the first page, Sharratt creates a voice that feels authentic to the time while making for beautiful, engaging reading.

Language in historical fiction is a fine line between staying true to the era while being readable to us modern folks. Writing with patience and persistence is key. Willingness to experiment with different styles and structures is a must. Reading wonderful historical novels helps. And Etymology Online is a blessing.

23

WHAT DID YOU SAY? DIALOGUE IN HISTORICAL FICTION

The historical novel gives us perspective on our modern lives and helps us connect with the story, which we are continuing ourselves.
~Mary Pope Osborne

Dialogue is another problem we see at *The Copperfield Review*. Let me explain.

In the chapter "Did That Word Exist Then?" I talked about language and word choice as a way to add atmosphere to historical fiction. The same applies to dialogue. As writers of historical fiction, we want to pull readers into the historical worlds we've created, and just as language can pull readers out of a story, so can wordy or stilted dialogue. It isn't necessary to perfectly mimic the way people spoke during whatever era we're writing about. We want our dialogue to reflect elements of the era but, as with word choice and sentence structure, our dialogue needs to be accessible to modern readers. Unwieldy, exaggerated dialogue does the opposite. At *Copperfield*, we've turned away pieces because the dialogue kept us from enjoying the story. The opposite is also true. Well-written dialogue can be a great way to pull readers into our historical worlds. As with language, there is a middle ground between staying true to the past and making our dialogue relatable to modern-day readers.

Dialogue shouldn't mimic the way people speak—either then or now. Today with our ums and ahs and other place-holders, to write the way we speak means it would take a page to get through a sentence. In the past, people were, let's say superfluous with their words, or at least they were with the written word. Read primary sources from the Victorian era, for example, and you'll see what looks like excessive language for the most simple thought. There's nothing inherently wrong with that—it's just that language styles go in and out of fashion like clothing.

Keep in mind that the point of dialogue is to give us insights into our characters and move the plot forward. Always. If a speech isn't necessary to understanding character or plot then it isn't necessary. Remove it. No matter how much you love the conversation, the unnecessary lines of dialogue—"Howdy! How are you today? Haven't seen you in a while. Where have you been?"—need to go.

Jump right into the meat of the conversation. When we're eavesdropping (not that we do such things, of course) we're not interested in the bland, every day stuff. We want to hear the juicy gossip. Dialogue is the same. What is the juicy part of the conversation? What do readers need to know to under-stand your characters, their problems, and their attitudes towards each other and the world? The best dialogue is stripped of all unessential elements, even in historical fiction. Keep dialogue simple. Even readers of historical fiction, who tend to love more details than readers of other genres, have only so much patience for awkward dialogue.

Also, be aware of writing in dialect. We see this a lot in the Old West or World War II stories sent to *The Copperfield Review*. I find having to decipher dialogue written in dialect a pain. My main man, Dickens, wrote a lot of his dialogue in dialect, and I don't like reading his dialect any more than I like reading it from anyone else. As with other aspects of language, try to find the rhythm, the cadence of the speech patterns without making the dialect read like a puzzle. If you're looking for examples of how to write historical dialogue, again, there are some wonderful historical novelists who do it very well. Look for some examples written about the era in which your story is set.

As it happens, I enjoy writing dialogue. Though it can be one of the most difficult aspects of fiction writing to master, I learned a trick that helped shape my dialogue writing for the better.

As I said earlier, I spent some time wanting to write screenplays. While I was at university I took a few screenwriting classes and worked at a film production company in "The Industry" otherwise known as Hollywood. Screenwriting itself wasn't for me, but one important lesson I took away from that experience is how to write dialogue. Studying screenwriting is the greatest gift novelists can give themselves since screenwriters, the good ones at least, understand how to pare dialogue down to its most essential parts. If you read the screenplays for your favorite films, you might be surprised at how little dialogue there actually is. Characters rarely give long speeches in TV or film unless there is a specific need for that speech.

A quick internet search will reveal a number of screenplays you can read for free. I typed "Screenplay Examples" into my search engine and a bunch of free-to-read screenplays popped up. Read them. Take notes. If you look up screenplays for your favorite movies you may only find extracts, but even a snippet is enough for you to see how dialogue is written. When I was taking screenwriting classes, the professors took great pains to teach us that we needed to keep our dialogue on point. One professor was adamant that it was rare for a character to say more than two lines at a time and anything more than two lines was considered a speech. That's it. Two lines.

Think about the last conversation you had with someone. When you're in the middle of a conversation, most of the time you only say a sentence or two before the other person chimes in. Maybe the more talkative amongst you say more than that, but in the course of daily conversations we really don't say much before someone else starts speaking. A friend of mine once said we only listen to people talk so we know what to say when it's our turn to speak. I think there's some truth to that. We're always interrupting each other and butting in, more interested in sharing our own thoughts than listening to what others are saying. Why should our characters be any different?

Another point to consider is that we do not always speak in complete sentences. Once you learn to pay attention to how people really speak, and once you become attuned to the dialogue in TV and film, you realize that people often speak in snippets. Even in historical fiction, if you want your dialogue to have the feel of an authentic conversation, you should take care that not everything your characters say is a perfectly constructed sentence.

See if you can find the screenplays for your favorite historical TV shows or movies. My favorites are the ones adapted from great works of literature written by Andrew Davies, who, in my mind at least, is one of the greatest screenwriters when it comes to adapting the classics. I also love Emma Thompson's adaptation of *Sense and Sensibility*. Granted, such screenplays have a head start since the original books were written by some of the greatest authors in the English language. Whichever historical screenplays you read, you'll see how the era is brought to life through the characters' words. You'll see what the characters say aloud and what they leave out or imply.

Now I have a hearing loss and I always turn on the captioning when I'm watching TV so I don't blast everyone else out of the house, but captioning works well for anyone who wants a better idea of what dialogue looks like. If you turn on the captioning while watching a historical TV show or film, you can see how much, or how little, the characters say. You can also see how the words and the acting come together to create the story in real time, which is something you won't get from reading the screenplay alone.

One thing I've learned from teaching creative writing workshops is that sometimes people think that because they are writing a novel their dialogue should be longer or wordier than it would appear in a screenplay. Generally speaking, that's not true. You want to keep your dialogue moving— even in a novel, and even in historical fiction.

The same professor who told my class that anything longer than two lines is a speech also said that the best actors, the ones worth their weight in beans, prefer less dialogue because they can do a lot with a few words. Our readers can do a lot with a few words too. People who love to read fiction enjoy filling in the blanks. Readers want to figure some things out for themselves, but they need white space on the page to do that. They need room to think. Filling in every little detail isn't necessary, in dialogue or description. Let your readers discover a character's hidden intention between the pause in their words. Readers become more invested in novels when they are allowed to participate in the story as it happens.

Once, a student in one of my creative writing classes asked me if the books for plays might also be helpful in learning how to write dialogue. My answer was maybe, depending on the playwright, but screenplays for TV and film are better.

In plays, characters speak more since theater is a language-based medium whereas TV and film are more visual mediums. Arthur Miller's *The Crucible* was helpful to me when I was writing about the Salem Witch Trials, but then Miller was a master of dialogue. Other playwrights (still, no names) don't have Miller's knack for getting to the heart of the matter. Yes, there are longer speeches in *The Crucible* because it's a play, but for the most part Miller had his characters say their bit and move on. It certainly doesn't hurt to look at the books of plays that interest you. The books could prove useful for reasons beyond dialogue.

Like everything else, writing strong dialogue comes with study and practice, but please do make sure your dialogue reads true. Although we are writing historical fiction, we don't want to drag our stories down with overly verbose, boring conversations.

If you would like to study how to write dialogue for screenplays, some books I can recommend that have been useful to me are *Making a Good Script Great* by Linda Seger, *Writing the Screenplay TV and Film* by Alan A. Armer, and *The Screenwriter's Bible* by David Trottier.

24

THE VALUE OF DIVERSITY

Language alone protects us from the scariness of things with no names. Language alone is meditation.
~Toni Morrison

Will our stories include people who are not entirely like us? As storytellers, we need to look honestly at all stories. History is not quaint or kind. History is not *Leave it to Beaver*. History is tough, brutal even. As historical novelists, will we face the discomforts head on, ignore them, or work around them?

I read an article on the Mythcreants website about why historical accuracy isn't a reason to exclude diversity in our writing. Yet we hear that excuse all the time from novelists, screenwriters, and others. My favorite show, *Downton Abbey*, received some grief for not including people of color, and the show's executives gave that exact excuse—historical accuracy. Lord Grantham and his ilk wouldn't have known people of color so the show didn't include any, that is until enough people complained. Finally, writer Julian Fellowes found a way to include a Black American jazz singer, for a few episodes anyway.

As writers of historical fiction, we should consider challenging ourselves past our comfort zones and including diverse characters in our fiction. But this leads us to another question. Do we have the right to write about people who are different from ourselves? Everyone has their own opinion on the subject, and so do I. I think that yes, we do have that right as long as we make a deliberate effort not to write in a stereotypical manner. So now we must ask whether or not we can be sensitive to different cultures, beliefs, and ways of being. Sometimes we don't know what we don't know about people, and that's okay, as long as we continue learning about people with different experiences than our own.

Maya Angelou said that we are more alike than we are different. Beneath language, beneath culture, or anything else we use to define others as different, there is an inherent sense of humanness that all people share. Carl Jung called it the Collective Unconscious. Maybe if we use that as our springboard, the idea that our characters—no matter who they are, no matter what era they live in, no matter the color of their skin or their religion or their sexual orientation—have an inherent sense of humanness, then the idea of reading or writing about diverse characters won't be so scary. If we approach historical fiction from the point of view that people are more alike than they are different, then maybe we can make the push to include diverse characters—that are not stereotypical—in our stories.

Writing about diverse people doesn't mean that our characters should hold hands and sing folk songs. If we're honest about history, we need to acknowledge that there have always been the oppressors and the oppressed. Equally, there have always been those who could sympathize with those who are different from themselves. All stories should be valued, and all stories should be remembered. Storytelling is the best way to learn about those who seem, on the surface at least, to be different from us. As readers and writers, we believe in the power of storytelling. We must, or why else would we spend so many hours reading and writing stories?

I made the decision to write about characters that are different from me because first, I don't want to stifle my creativity in any way, and second, I don't want to gloss over elements of history that are difficult. If I'm making a decision to paint the past through writing historical fiction, then I need to write stories that are sometimes uncomfortable.

For example, in *Her Loving Husband's Curse* I wrote about the removal of Native American tribes during the Trail of Tears. I chose to have Cherokee characters because I couldn't tell the story without them. One of my goals when writing historical fiction is to inspire readers with enough curiosity about the era that they seek nonfiction historical accounts. I couldn't give a detailed analysis of the westward expulsion of the Native American tribes within the limitations of my story structure, but I hoped that readers would become interested enough that they wanted to read more. There are many lessons we can learn from the Trail of Tears. As a society we still suffer from intolerance, ignorance, and greed, the traits that allowed the westward expulsion in the first place.

In *Her Loving Husband's Return* I wrote about the detainment of Japanese-Americans in the Manzanar Relocation Camp and I included Japanese-American characters because, again, I couldn't tell the story without them. My goal when writing characters that are different from me is to always write about them with integrity and respect.

In *Down Salem Way* I didn't feel comfortable writing about

James' father's mercantile business without addressing the fact that the business was involved, even indirectly, in piracy and the slave trade. Whether John Wentworth is personally involved in the slave trade is a matter of inconsequence since the rum he sells is traded for human beings. Although the slave trade is not a huge part of the story, to talk about life in Colonial America without acknowledging ties to the slave trade would be glossing over one of the most essential elements of the birth of the United States. I didn't touch on the slave trade in great detail because if I included more about the slave trade I would have lost control of the narrative, which would have meant the death of the story I wanted to tell about the Salem Witch Trials. The slave trade in the earliest Colonial American days isn't a subject that has been frequently tackled in historical fiction, and I for one would love to see a novelist bring that to life.

What can we do to promote diversity in historical fiction? As writers, we can consider how we might include diverse people in our stories. As readers, we can make an effort to read historical novels that are written by or about diverse people. The answer, really, is that we all need to push ourselves past our comfort zones. The more we can learn about each other, the truth and not the stereotypes, the more we can understand each other. The more we can understand each other, the more we can build bridges toward each other.

And if you see a story that should be told but hasn't, or if you're unhappy with the way others have told certain stories, well, Toni Morrison taught us that if there is a book you want to read and it has not been written, then you must write it. Don't wait for someone else to tell the stories that need to be shared. More needs to be done for the stories of people who have been traditionally marginalized. As Isabelle Allende said, "Write what should not be forgotten." As historical novelists, we have the unique privilege of keeping stories, all stories, alive.

25

WE ARE NOT HISTORIANS

Truth is stranger than fiction, but it is because Fiction is obliged to stick to possibilities; Truth isn't.
   ~Mark Twain

How much leeway can the writer of historical fiction take with the facts? As the executive editor of *The Copperfield Review*, I'm asked that question frequently. Here's my answer: it's up to authors to decide how they are going to intertwine the history with the fiction they are creating. Ultimately, historical stories must be believable. Readers must believe that they have traveled to that era through the magic of the written word.

Here's a point that isn't often addressed when we discuss historical accuracy in historical fiction: whose narrative are we using as the basis for the history in our fiction? Which biographies are we studying? Which historians are we looking to for information?

When it comes to history, we've been handed a specific

bill of goods that may or may not be based on fact. I'm a huge fan of Lucy Worsley, an English historian. Worsley has a fabulous TV series where she debunks myths about historical figures, myths that have become so accepted that they are unquestioned as part of the narrative of these important people. For example, there is no evidence that Marie Antoinette said, "Let them eat cake." The phrase was attributed to her years after her death by her enemies. She was an astute political thinker, better than her husband, in fact, but that information about this fascinating woman was pushed aside in favor of portraying her as a selfish, materialistic gold-digger who only cared about her own well being while the French people suffered. How many biographies, novels, and films have portrayed her in just this way?

In scholarship, it's accepted that everyone has biases, and scholars are trained to acknowledge their biases in their research. The Merriam-Webster dictionary defines bias as an inclination of temperament or outlook, especially a personal and sometimes unreasoned judgment. Biases are often based on our influences and perceptions. Historical novelists have biases too. What are your biases, and how are those biases affecting how you share the history in your fiction? Are you unable to see Henry VIII beyond that of a monster who beheaded inconvenient wives? Are you unable to accept the social mores of the era you're writing about so you make your characters more modern in their beliefs? We are not historians, but it can be helpful to recognize our own biases, our own blindspots, so that we can understand why we are shaping the history the way we are.

So then which history do we tell? This leads us back to considering our sources. Who is writing the history books we are using for our research? Does this person have an agenda outside that of historian? Newer biographies and nonfiction accounts tend to be more valued since they contain the most recent scholarship, but even so you need to look at who is writing the history. I'm partial to the research of university professors, but even some professors may support an agenda that has nothing to do with the historical record—or, in other words, their interpretation of the source material is more about their biases than the historical record itself. Even so, most historical eras have respected historians, and those historians would be my first line of defense. When I began researching the Salem Witch Trials, Marilynne K. Roach kept popping up as a respected historian and she became my primary resource for both *Her Dear & Loving Husband* and *Down Salem Way*.

For writers who feel the need to fiddle with the historical record for whatever reason, I won't say it's wrong to do. I've done it myself. Sometimes it's a silly change, like the color of men's clothing during the Victorian era. When Dickens was a young writer in the 1830s, brightly colored waistcoats were all the rage. By the 1870s, when my Hembry stories take place, men opted for more somber colors. However, when I wrote *Christmas at Hembry Castle* I wanted Frederick, the Earl of Staton, to wear a brightly colored waistcoat at his Christmas festivities so I used my autonomy as the costume designer and put him in one. I made one or two other minor changes that represented how things were done earlier in the Victorian era since *Christmas at Hembry Castle* is a homage to *A Christmas Carol*, which was published in 1843.

If you're making larger changes, however, the former history teacher in me is compelled to suggest adding a note about it at the end of your novel. This way your readers know that you know that you fudged some of the facts. Historical fiction readers are savvy. Many are familiar with the era they are reading about. Maybe they have read a lot of historical fiction about the era or they are so fascinated by the time that they have read nonfiction accounts. Some of those readers will be annoyed that you changed some things, but I find that most will understand. As long as your characters and your plot are entertaining, they'll forgive a nudge here and there. However, I don't think we should make massive changes to the history. If we aren't going to adhere to the essence of the historical record then why write historical fiction? You can choose to write alternative historical fiction instead.

Perhaps the task of the historical storyteller is to make the history interesting enough so readers will become curious and want to read nonfiction accounts. Some of the greatest compliments I've received about my historical fiction is when readers say they became interested in the Salem Witch Trials, the Trail of Tears, and the Women's Suffrage Movement after reading my novels. I always include a few of my favorite research books in my Author's Notes so these readers have an idea where they can begin such a journey.

Having said all this, some authors simply want to have fun with their stories. Julia Quinn, author of the *Bridgerton* books that have been all the rage due to the Netflix series, said that she has been dinged by the accuracy police since some historical aspects of her Regency romances don't ring true to those in the know. If your intention is simply to write an entertaining story, that's okay. Write the story you want to write. After all, some readers are more interested in the story (in Quinn's case, juicy Regency romances) than they are in historical accuracy.

There is a difference between fudging historical accuracy and filling in the blanks where there is no historical record, or only a flimsy one. There are many gaps in historical scholarship where little or nothing is known about specific people, places, or events, especially the earlier back you go. When you discover these gaps through your research, this is where you can allow your imagination to truly soar. You aren't changing anything. You're simply imagining what that event or person was like when we have no historical record to tell us. Maggie O'Farrell's *Hamnet* is a fine example. We know very little about Shakespeare's life, but O'Farrell, through extensive research into sixteenth-century England and a vivid imagination, recreates what might have happened to Shakespeare's son Hamnet, whose death is believed to have inspired the playwright's *Hamlet*. *I, Tituba: Black Witch of Salem* by Maryse Condé is another example of using a vivid imagination to fill in the blanks about Tituba, the slave who was accused of witchcraft and arrested during the Salem Witch Trials.

You'll need to decide how closely you want to stick to the facts about your chosen era; however, I would suggest that many of the most popular historical novelists do meticulous research and stick largely to what is known as a way to shape their characters and plot. If liberties are taken, they are for the sake of the story and they are not glaringly obvious.

Since we are not historians, we can take those liberties. The primary job of the historical storyteller is not simply to educate readers with facts about the past. Our job is to tell entertaining tales set in specific times.

26

IN CONCLUSION

The best moments in reading are when you come across something – a thought, a feeling, a way of looking at things – which you had thought special and particular to you. Now here it is, set down by someone else, a person you have never met, someone even who is long dead. And it is as if a hand has come out and taken yours.

~Alan Bennett, *The History Boys*

As readers and writers of historical fiction, we are drawn to the past and the present simultaneously. We understand that the past has helped to create our world today, and, as Oliver Wendell Holmes Jr. stated, we need only look back to know what will happen tomorrow.

Writing historical fiction provides its own particular joy. The joy comes from the knowledge that we have taken interesting moments from the past and made them accessible to readers who love well-written stories. There is satisfaction in sharing our love of history with others. Too many people find history pointless, even boring, but those of us who love historical fiction know better.

For me, historical fiction serves as a TARDIS of sorts, allowing me to travel through space to any given point in time. With fiction you get sights, sounds, emotions, tension. That's why I write historical fiction. It uses a different part of the brain than when I'm writing nonfiction. I enjoy writing history-based nonfiction, and I enjoy reading it, but sometimes history books feel like a list of names, dates, and facts, which is not always interesting to me, even when it's a subject I want to learn about.

When I'm writing historical fiction, I want to bring the reader back in time with me. The more I feel as if I've traveled to that era, and the more I enjoy my visit there, the more my readers will enjoy the ride. A well-written historical story is both an escape from our current time as well as a lens through which we can examine the world in which we live.

Weaving fact and fiction is a creative process. The idea that writing is either a business or a creative pursuit is a false dichotomy set up by those who think in black or white, this or that, right or wrong. As I've learned, and perhaps you have too, things are rarely that simple. Most things fall somewhere in between the two extremes. You don't have to choose between being a creative writer and a writer who writes to make a living. You can be both.

Even if you don't think of your own writing as artistic, it is. Creating a world inhabited by believable characters who deal with believable problems is as artistic as it gets. Acknowledging your creativity does not make you less of a marketer, or a publisher, or a business person. Embracing your imagination is how you will sustain your writing career since you'll always know how to refill your creative well. If you are looking to write historical fiction, if you are looking to weave together facts from the past in a way that will capture readers' attention, then you are a creative person. Your creativity will see you through the challenges of a writing career in a way that the business aspects may not.

I ditto Anne Lamott's experience, which she speaks of in *Bird by Bird*, in that when I teach creative writing I find that some of my students have unrealistic expectations about the ease of creating a profitable writing career. Yes, some writers make a fabulous living selling books. Some writers make a living selling some books, selling some courses, speaking engagements, podcasting, vlogging, blogging, or all of the above. Some writers make a living selling nonfiction books, which subsidizes their fiction writing. Some (probably most) writers have day jobs. This is true of both traditionally published and independently published authors.

I will root for anyone determined to turn their dreams into reality. I certainly have. However, a writing career isn't easy, and it can take time to create the career you want. I wrote three novels, countless short stories, and numerous articles between the years 1994 and 2011, which is when I had my first bestselling novel. Even with my limited math skills, I can tell you that's 17 years, which is a long time to do something for the love of it. Even though I had my ups and downs over nearly two decades, in the end I wrote because I had to. I couldn't live peacefully with myself if I didn't. Writing is the only time I feel like I'm in tune with the universe, when I know I'm doing what I was put here to do.

If you're driven to write historical fiction, then write historical fiction. It may take time to create the career you want, but if you continue honing your craft and growing in your skills, you'll get there in the end.

. . .

I hope you have found some information in this book that is of use to you. I hope you have discovered a few ideas that will prompt your creativity to soar.

Writing historical fiction shares many traits with writing any genre of fiction. It's the history that makes historical fiction come alive, and it's the history that keeps devoted readers coming back. I've shared some of the tricks I've learned over 20 years of writing, teaching, and editing historical fiction. Now the rest is up to you. What era are you going to write about? How will you conduct your research? Who will people your story and how will you weave the historical record into your narrative? What problems will your people face? What style of language will you use?

The most important skill writers need to learn is to trust themselves. Trust your vision. Your voice. Your love of history and your passion for the written word. That doesn't mean you ignore helpful advice or ideas. It does mean you stop looking to everyone else for the answers you already have. You know what story you want to tell. The people shouting about how you must write are exactly that—people like you and me—sharing what worked for them. But only you can discover your own best writing practices. When it comes to taking writing advice, which is all this book is—advice—I've learned to take what works for me and leave the rest behind. I'm not making proclamations about how you should write historical fiction. I've shared what has inspired me over the years, which in turn, I hope, inspires you.

The only way to learn how to write historical fiction is by writing historical fiction. Start by getting your ideas out of your head and onto paper or screen. Don't skimp on the brainstorming or the prewriting. Stories are born from ideas, and you need a lot of ideas to work with. Allow yourself time to daydream. Experiment. Seek inspiration from your favorite authors and historical novels. Try different voices and different points of view. This is your story. Tell it your way.

Writing historical fiction is one of my greatest joys in this life. I hope you experience something similar as you embark on telling your own historical tales. Through historical fiction we can learn about the past from engaging characters and fascinating events. Through historical fiction we can see where we have been and where we are going.

AUTHOR'S NOTES

If you'd like to continue your journey with writing historical fiction, you can find the free workbook here: https://dl.bookfunnel.com/d56pkm6dgn. The workbook is meant to be a fun way to interact with the prompts you have read in the book.

I must thank the many readers and contributors at *The Copperfield Review*. Twenty-one years ago I came up with the crazy idea of creating an e-zine specifically for historical fiction. At the time, I thought, "Who is even going to read this?" A lot of people, it turns out. People found it, read it, shared it with their friends, decided to write for it, and told more friends, who then decided to write for it. Some found us through literary journal listings. Mainly, people have discovered us through word of mouth, which is the best publicity of all. I've learned a lot about the art and craft of writing historical fiction through my work as an editor. In case you were wondering, yes, *The Copperfield Review* is named after Dickens' novel.

I must also thank my writing students. Every time I teach writing I learn more than I teach, I'm sure of it.

I'm consistently amazed at the communications I receive from readers all over the world who have enjoyed my historical fiction. As someone who only ever wanted to tell stories, it has been a dream come true. Thank you.

If you're looking for other books to inspire your writing, I can recommend the following. These titles are oldies but goodies, but to this day I haven't found anything better: *Writing Down the Bones* and *Wild Mind* by Natalie Goldberg and *Bird by Bird* by Anne Lamott. I've read the books by Goldberg and Lamott so many times I've digested their messages into my bloodstream.

For specifics on the writing craft, *The Art and Craft of Novel Writing* by Oakley Hall and *How to Write and Sell Your First Novel* by Oscar Collier are good places to start.

ABOUT THE AUTHOR

Meredith Allard is the author of the bestselling paranormal historical Loving Husband Trilogy. Her sweet Victorian romance, When It Rained at Hembry Castle, was named a best historical novel by IndieReader. Painting the Past: A Guide for Writing Historical Fiction was named a #1 New Release in Authorship and Creativity Self-Help by Amazon. When she isn't writing she's teaching writing, and she has taught writing to students ages five to 75.

Meredith is the Founder and Executive Editor of *The Copperfield Review*, an award-winning literary journal for readers and writers of historical fiction. She received her B.A. and M.A. degrees in English from CSU Northridge and her Ph.D. from the University of Nevada, Las Vegas. She loves books, cats, and coffee, though not always in that order. She lives in Las Vegas, Nevada. Visit Meredith online at www.meredithallard.com.

ALSO BY MEREDITH ALLARD

Christmas at Hembry Castle

Down Salem Way

Her Dear & Loving Husband

Her Loving Husband's Curse

Her Loving Husband's Return

The Loving Husband Trilogy Complete Box Set

The Loving Husband Series

That You Are Here

Victory Garden

When It Rained at Hembry Castle

The Window Dresser and Other Stories

Woman of Stones

Made in the USA
Las Vegas, NV
27 September 2021